Camels, Skulls, and Cobras

A Wild Ride Across India

Text, illustrations, maps, and photos by Jim Wiltens

Deer Crossing Press
Redwood City, California

Cover photo provided by permission from Reuters News Service:
Dan Wright and Jim Wiltens seated with their camels, Raika and
Sam, the Taj Mahal is in the background.

Back cover author photo: Susan Jones.

Library of Congress Control Number: 2008922222
$14.95 Pbk

ISBN: 978-0-938525-09-7

First Printing 2008

Deer Crossing Press
690 Emerald Hill Rd.
Redwood City, CA 94061

Printed in the United States of America

10   9   8   7   6   5   4   3   2   1

Dedication

Visvajeet "Bubbles" Singh and I met through a number of amazing coincidences. When we discovered each other, he told me, "I would ride with you if I could, but I have too many commitments. So I will be part of your adventure by helping you with whatever you need." At first I was cautious in accepting his help. After all we had just met. As the days went by I discovered that he was as enthusiastic about the expedition as we were. His hospitality humbled me. He and his hotel staff at the Harasar Haveli did everything possible to help us prepare for the expedition. If I had to make a list of all the arrangements and advice Bubbles provided it would take many pages. He provided jeep transportation into the desert, bailed us out when we got into tight spots, met us along the trail to check how we were doing, put us up with relatives at his fortress in the desert, shipped equipment, set up a press conference. He introduced us to Pane Singh, a retired military man much respected in the desert community who would help us with our camel purchase; Ranveer Singh, whose generosity made our trip go much smoother; Katea-ram, our camel guru; Iqrar, our interpreter; Vijay, our guide in Bikaner; Gurav, our autorickshaw driver . . . the list goes on. My adventure buddy, Dan, and I agreed that Bubbles's friendship is what made our trip a success. Thank you, Bubbles.

Books by Jim Wiltens

Individual Tactics in Waterpolo

Edible and Poisonous Plants of Northern California

*No More Nagging, Nit-picking, & Nudging: A Guide to
Motivating, Inspiring, and Influencing Kids Aged 10–18*

Goal Express! The Five Secrets of Goal-Setting Success

Memory Smart: Nine Memory Skills Every Grade Schooler Needs

Camels, Skulls, and Cobras: A Wild Ride Across India

Contents

Slipping Under the Barbwire

It was innocent fun, two youngsters pushing and shoving—a play-ground scuffle. As the responsible adult in charge, I didn't think much of it. Then one drew blood. That's when things got ugly. Saddam hooked Milagro around the neck and slammed him to the ground. If getting thrown to the ground didn't knock the wind out of Milagro, having Saddam crash down on top of him surely did. Showing no mercy, Saddam splayed his legs in good wrestler fashion and worked a knee over Milagro's throat to suffocate him. "No, no, no!" I yelled running towards the fight. I yanked off my hat and started swatting at Saddam. Bad move. Saddam swung his head at me. His head, as big as my chest and connected to a four-foot long neck, swished by like a sledgehammer. Fourteen hundred pounds of enraged camel, the bad boy of the herd, Saddam was not going to be stopped by a whack with a hat. In panic I watched Milagro suffo-cating. Gary was going to blow a gasket if I let one of his camels die.

Gary Jackson owns the Nevada Camel Company. We met the previous year when I came to take camel riding lessons in prepara-tion for an upcoming expedition. Now I was back in Stage Coach, Nevada, sagebrush capital of the world, to baby-sit his camels. Gary needed to attend a wedding. I needed camel experience. So, with Gary's permission, I parked my truck next to the camel corral. The plan was to live out of my truck for a week while caring for the camels 24 hours a day. The way things were going, it looked like part of that care would include burying a camel.

Think, think, think. I looked about frantically. Then I saw it. I sprinted across the corral. *Grab and scoop.* Rushing back towards the brawl, I took aim. I'd only get one shot. I heaved a bucket of water at Saddam's head. Direct hit! That got his attention. Sputtering, he lurched to his feet, forcing me to dive under the fence. It wasn't over. He glared at me. A sound came from his throat, as if he was bellowing while gargling a bathtub full of Listerine. Then he turned back towards Milagro. Poor Milagro had gotten his hump wedged under a fence during the fight and was stuck. Saddam moved in for the kill. I raced around the corral to where grenade sized food pellets were stored and started lobbing them over the fence. The resounding "thunks" brought Saddam's head up. He looked at the food, then at Milagro, and then back to the food. He made a decision when he saw other members of the herd start gobbling up the pellets. Food overcame his murderous mood. Reluctantly, he turned away from Milagro and trotted to the far side of the corral for an early lunch.

Milagro, still wedged under the fence, frantically kicked his legs. I planted my boots against his hump, and holding onto one of the corral posts for leverage, I pushed. Slowly, he inched out from under the rail. Finally freed, he staggered to his feet. Other than several bright red gashes on his legs and flanks where Saddam had bitten him, Milagro was fine. You would think he would want revenge, a little pay back against Saddam. Maybe he might even consider thanking me. Neither option appealed to Milagro. When it comes to food, camels are single-minded. He loped over to feed with the rest of the herd as if nothing had happened. I, on the other hand, walked shakily over to my truck and slumped on the tailgate clutching my cowboy hat.

Sitting on the back of the truck waiting for the adrenalin jitters to wear off, a voice hissed in my ear, *Whoa, that was close. And this is only the beginning. This is a bad sign. Better back out.* That worrisome voice has followed me around since I was a kid.

When I was nine my family moved. In terms of distance, it was a short jump. We went from city life in Berkeley, California, to a small subdivision in Moraga ten miles away, surrounded by

A deadly camel brawl. Clockwise from top left, three camels mix it up. Then Saddam separates out Milagro. Saddam arches over Milagro's back and grabs a leg in his teeth. Saddam throws his opponent to the ground and climbs on top to suffocate him.

thousands of acres of rolling hills. It felt like moving to the wilderness. A barbwire fence across the street separated our new house from the unknown hills beyond. The first time I slipped between those strands of wire, the voice tagged along. It nagged me to return to safety. Had I listened I would have missed some great childhood adventures. Following a creek that vanished into a dark tunnel filled with mind goblins and coming out alive on the other side; finding that I had Superman's ability to leap over a tall pasture fence when chased by a herd of cattle. Then there was the discovery of a far off lake where I experienced the electric tingle that arced from fishing line to spine when a blue gill hit my hook.

None of those memories would be mine if I had obeyed the voice. It was the voice of fear. Some people say fear is good. It keeps you from doing stupid stuff. Like the time I leaped off our roof. I was ten and thought that a surplus army parachute the size of a small throw rug would protect me. I smacked into the ground, the chute still draped over my shoulders. Nothing got broken, but maybe a little more fear would have kept me from jumping.

So is fear a friend or foe? It's a foe when it predicts the future with no options but failure, embarrassment, and rejection. When it makes statements like, *Don't do that, dumb, dumb, dumb, never been done before, not going to be done now,* then it is the great thought blocker. One of its nastier side effects is panic. In its "friendly" mode, it asks questions, *Can you handle it? Are you paying attention? Have you planned and prepared?* It not only asks questions, it expects an answer like, "Oh yeah, I filled a suitcase with rocks, tied a parachute to the handles, and pushed it off the roof. It hit the ground hard. Guess I need a bigger parachute." Friendly fear is big on planning. That's why I was spending a week camping out with camels. Dealing with angry camels was part of the preparation I needed to answer fear's questions. Soon I would be "leaping off the roof" and "slipping under the barbwire" yet again.

Adventure Buddies

Dan Wright is my adventure buddy. We met when he came to work at the children's summer camp I own in California: Deer Crossing Camp. At Deer Crossing, Dan was hired as our lead rock climbing instructor. His home base is England, but he has guided climbing trips across Europe, Nepal, India, and Kashmir. His decision to work at Deer Crossing was based on the recommendation of another instructor from our camp, also a Briton. "Dan, the climbing is brilliant. There are granite walls around this summer camp that have never been roped. A climber would have to have biscuits for brains not to love it." When Dan arrived, his expectations were met. "Do you know how hard it is to find an unclimbed face in Europe?" Dan asked. "This is going to be a giggle" (which in Brit slang means "great fun").

While I often enjoy friendships with a number of my instructors, Dan's can-do enthusiasm was particularly appealing. He loved our wilderness camp and often came up with ideas to make it better, such as theme nights, where everyone came in craft-room created costumes. Campers wore cowboy outfits and Roman togas, and Dan showed up in a white suit complete with cardboard tie. He also introduced us to Hollywood climbing. Hollywood climbing challenges campers to climb incredibly difficult pitches of rock. It is also completely safe. The climbers are on a horizontal rather than a vertical surface. They set protection, belay (secure position), and make moves without any possibility of a fall. It is called Hollywood climbing because that is how actors can appear to climb an impossible pitch in movies. Actually, they are lying on the rock. Trick photography makes it look vertical. Then there was the time he taught campers a New Zealand Maori war dance. It was hilarious. Twenty campers followed Dan's lead as he stomped his feet, stuck out his tongue, and chanted a Maori war song.

The campers loved Dan's energy. So did I. We often stayed up late at night discussing climbing, teaching techniques, motivational psychology, and our favorite topic—adventure. As I got to know Dan, I found out that adventure was in his bloodline.

"My grandparents moved from Britain to the island of Sri Lanka off the tip of India before the outbreak of World War II," explained Dan in his proper British accent. (At camp, Dan was affectionately known as "Posh Dan" due to his lord-of-the-manor accent.) "When the war started, my grandfather joined a rifle regiment and became an intelligence officer in Burma. My grandmother worked for British Intelligence in Dehra Dun, India. After the war they became missionaries and moved to the shores of Lake Victoria in Tanzania, Africa. At Christmas I remember our family using Swahili phrases around the dinner table. Sometimes my grandmother told stories about people she had known, like Heinrich Harrer who would later go on to become the teacher and friend of the Dalai Lama, the religious leader of Tibet. She talked about three-day steam train rides across the African bush, where they saw zebras racing the train and lions lying next to the tracks. I desperately wanted to follow in their footsteps. When I was eighteen, I went to India alone and fell in love with the people and the culture. Ever since then I have found travel to be my greatest passion. When did the adventure bug bite you?"

Thinking for a moment I replied, "Two things. My uncle Bob and the most boring/exciting summer of my life. My uncle wanted to be an adventure filmmaker. Once he bought a jeep to explore the Mojave Desert. He got stuck in the sand, visited abandoned gold mines, where pickaxes, ore carts, and shovels were laying about like the miners had taken a break for lunch. He brought me a huge quartz crystal he'd found in one of the mines. He'd tell these great stories. Sometimes I tagged along on his adventures. When I was eight he asked if I wanted to visit some of his friends. We drove up the coast of California and turned off on a road that dead-ended at the sea cliffs. It was a vertical drop to the ocean below. We tied a rope to the car bumper and slid down the face of the cliff to a small beach. There were a bunch of his "friends" lying on the sand like rolls of carpet. It was a colony of sea lions. We snuck up on them by crawling on our bellies in the sand. We got close enough to smell their fishy breath. When they finally sensed our presence, they stampeded towards the ocean. The beach shook like an earthquake, sea gulls were screaming, sand was flying everywhere. I loved it, but my Uncle found there was more money to be made in portrait photography. He gave up adventure film-making, but I never forgot those trips."

"And the most boring/exciting summer of your life?" asked Dan.

"Around seventh grade we moved into a rental in Los Altos, California, while our new home was being built," I said. "The move occurred in the summer, the worst time. There weren't any kids my age in the neighborhood and not much to do. The library became my closest friend. I read as many as two books a day. Some of my favorites were *My Side of the Mountain, Kon-Tiki,* and *Tarzan.* I would read an entire shelf of books and then move to the next shelf. That summer I fell asleep with dreams of crossing deserts, sailing oceans, climbing mountains, and poling through swamps.

My parents knew it was hard on me. Even though they were saving pennies to buy a new house, they scraped together the money to send me to a working horse ranch for two weeks. Going from tantalizing bookworm adventures to riding horses, stringing barbwire fences, learning to shoot, and sleeping under the stars was like the difference between a forty-watt light bulb and a Fourth of July fireworks display."

The more Dan and I talked, the more convinced we became that we needed to go on an adventure together.

False Start

During one of our evening chats, Dan posed a question.

"Mate, what 'da you know about elephants?"

"When they sneeze they use four boxes of Kleenex," I joked.

Dan ignored me, "Have you heard about the Englishman who rode an elephant across India?"

"Yes," I replied. "Didn't he write *Travels on My Elephant?*"

"You've read it?" Dan looked surprised.

"Yes. An Englishman, Mark Shand, buys a thirty-year-old elephant, Tara, and rides 800 miles from the Bay of Bengal across India to the great elephant bazaar on the Ganges River."

Dan looked at me in a calculating sort of way. "Whot' say, we do the same thing, but with a twist. Let's ride an elephant across India to Nepal."

It is said that the quality of your life is determined by the quality of the questions that you ask. Ask dull questions and suffer a dull life. Ask outrageous questions, and live an outrageous life. Dan's question was definitely outrageous. I knew nothing about elephants. I knew less about India and Nepal. The idea was simply too crazy to consider—but I did. I considered it, and I loved it.

Having Dan as an adventure buddy was a no-brainer. Where else would I find someone who would give up three months of a paying job that enables him to buy necessities like food and shelter in favor of dragging ill-mannered beasts across Asia? Actually I had two other reasons for partnering with Dan. One stems from something related to his birth.

Dan was born with a serious medical condition. The doctor told his mother, "Your son will never lead a normal life." Her newborn had an entrance for food to go in but no exit. He lacked important internal plumbing. Dan's parents were referred to a surgeon who told them about a new experimental procedure. When his parents consented, the surgeon accepted their baby as a human guinea pig. The operation involved cutting an opening, constructing a bowel from his intestines, and using stomach muscles to replace other missing parts. Dan is now famous for this operation. His baby pictures appear in medical journals. He's wearing a little black mask, an infant Lone Ranger, to preserve his privacy. Having spent a lifetime dealing with the sometimes-embarrassing side effects of this operation and realizing that surgery was necessary to save his life, Dan is not easily rattled by embarrassment. "Why be shy or embarrassed in life?" says Dan. "I'm supposed to be dead." Free of the fear of embarrassment means Dan is willing to ask anyone for anything. This is a valuable asset in an adventure buddy, especially for a guy like me, who is more easily flustered by embarrassing events.

The second reason for choosing Dan as an adventure buddy is that he doesn't ruminate. Camels ruminate. They cough up some plant material they've already swallowed and chew on it like a wad of gum—all day. Humans do something similar. Only they do it mentally. They puke up an annoying incident and chew on that. Maybe your friend brushes his teeth and spits on the place you were going to lay your bedroll. Even though he had no idea that was your future bedroll spot—the best spot on the planet for you to sleep—you think, *I don't get no respect.* You replay this incident over and over in your mind. As you chew on it your resentment grows. Eventually you want to spit on every sleeping spot at the next campsite—*pay back.* Fortunately Dan is not a ruminator. If something bugs him, he says something and then drops it.

So I had an adventure partner, and we had a tentative plan. But dreams do not always go according to plan. As I researched what it would take to put together an elephant ride across Asia, I added up the costs for buying an elephant, hiring a support crew, paying a veterinarian, buying a gazillion tons of elephant feed, renting two trucks to transport the feed, and purchasing fuel. The estimated cost was a half million dollars!

At this point, Dan suggested a revision to the plan.

"I really want to do this trip before I'm an old duffer," said Dan. "Raising a half million dollars is going to take a lot of time. What do you say we ride something smaller than an elephant?"

"Like what?"

"Well I have always wanted to go on a long caravan trip. They have camels in India. Let's put together our own caravan."

"What a great idea. We could follow one of the old trade routes, the silk road, across India."

That's all it took to switch from elephants to camels.

Of course it meant that I had to start researching a whole new area, dromedaries, the one-humped camels of India. Part of my expedition homework included watching the movie *Lawrence of Arabia*. In one scene the actor, Peter O'Toole, gallops across the desert riding on a long-gaited camel over undulating sand dunes, his swan-white robes flapping in the breeze. I was sold. We would gallop across India. We might even wear swan-white robes.

More tweaks were needed to finalize the plan.

"You know, since we won't be on a slow, plodding elephant, why don't we make the trip longer?" I suggested.

Dan nodded. "What do you have in mind?"

Going through my notes, I said, "In 1883, camels in Australia carried 770-pound packs 278 miles in 16 days. That's about 17 miles a day. And a camel researcher, Hilde Gauthier-Pilters, hired camels for four weeks covering 19 miles a day carrying 265-pound loads. We won't be carrying as much weight, so 20 miles a day is possible. In three months, including rest days, I think 1,500 miles is doable."

Tracing his finger over a map, Dan said, "Let's start near the India-Pakistan border in the Thar Desert, ride across India, head into Nepal, cross over the Himalayas, maybe make a side trip to Mt. Everest, then on to Lhasa, Tibet. About 1,500 miles."

"OK," I replied. "We've got a route. We've settled on transportation—camels. Now we need to figure out how we can incorporate Mahatma Gandhi's advice into our plan."

Mahatma Gandhi, the great Indian leader I was referring to, did not personally advise me. That's not likely, since he died over a half-century ago. My counsel and inspiration came from his writings. He said, "You must be the change you wish to see in the world." So Dan and I now asked, "How could we be part of a change that we wished to see in the world? How could our adventure help people?"

My first thought was literacy. I like spreading literacy. For example, when I paraglide in Mexico, jumping off volcanoes under what looks like a giant parachute, kids hang out in the landing zone. They offer to fold paragliders for twenty-five cents. When I land and the kids run up to me, I hold up a hand and say, *Momentito, niños* (I need a moment, kids). Then I rummage around in my flight pack and bring out one of the most powerful books on the planet, and say, "If you want to fold for me, you must read a paragraph out of this book." The book is *Captain Underpants*—in Spanish. If they can read a paragraph, I not only pay them, but also give them a book like *Captain Underpants* or *The Magic School Bus*. Now I offer my helpers a deal. "Want to fold for me again?" They always nod yes. "Then teach another kid to read a paragraph in your book. Do that, and I will pay each of you with cash and a book."

While I love spreading literacy, carrying a load of books on a camel didn't seem practical—too bulky, too heavy, and I don't read Hindi. I needed help coming up with an idea. After going through a list of acquaintances, I called Tom Kelley. Tom is the general manager of IDEO, a creative design company in Palo Alto, California. He's in the business of coming up with ideas.

Over lunch he asked, "Have you heard about the connection between light and literacy?"

"No," I replied.

"If you are a child in a poor third-world country, you work next to your parents in the fields during daylight hours. Your only chance for study is at night. Here's the problem. In many villages in Asia, they study by the flames of kerosene lamps."

Later I learned about all the drawbacks of kerosene lighting. In India alone, 2.5 million people suffer severe burns each year, primarily due to overturned kerosene lamps. It gets worse. Kerosene lamps are also unhealthy. Studying near the fumes of a kerosene lamp for one evening is equivalent to smoking two packs of cigarettes. Not a good thing for kids. This contributes to a high incidence of lung cancer in people who don't smoke. Plus kerosene is expensive. It costs fifty-two dollars a year, a lot of money for a poor villager.

Tom continued, "There's an organization, the *Light Up The World Foundation* (www.lutw.org), that installs healthy, self-sustaining, solar-powered light-emitting diodes (LEDs) in remote villages to replace kerosene lamps. These units are small and easily transported."

A light bulb—or should I say an LED—went off in my head. After lunch, I contacted Dr. Dave Irvine-Halliday, the founder of the *Light Up The World Foundation,* and discussed the possibility of a partnership. Thus was born our name, Caravan of Light. Our plan was to install solar-powered light systems along our route and promote what Dr. Irvine-Halliday calls, "the light-in-a-box system." We hoped to mount light systems in three villages along our route—one in India, one in Nepal, and one in Tibet. Dr. Irvine-Halliday sent us the hardware for the Indian leg of the trip. Two more light-in-a-box packages would be waiting for us in Nepal. More important, we would tell journalists about the benefits of spreading these light systems so that more people would become aware of the benefits.

The final part of the plan was to make the trip an educational experience. As a consultant working with gifted and talented education (GATE) programs in California, I wanted my students to be able to follow the journey. Using a laptop computer hooked up to a satellite phone and powered by solar panels, we would transmit journal entries from our expedition to a website (www.thecaravanoflight.com). We hoped that our Indiana Jones-style of adventure would hook students into reading our journal entries. These entries would also include information on the geography, culture, and science of the region we passed through. Dan added that he wanted to transmit live weekly updates of our progress to a British Broadcasting Corporation (BBC) radio station in Britain.

A Bright Future

The acceptance of some new technologies occurs faster in poor countries. Take the cell phone for example. When I visited South Africa years ago, while it seemed everyone had a cell phone, they were still uncommon in the U.S. The reason so many Africans had cell phones was that the traditional telephone system was in a horrible state of repair. Setting up telephone poles and stringing telephone wires is more difficult than maintaining the repeater stations that make cell phones work. In Africa, cell phones were more reliable than the traditional phone system. Everyone who could afford a phone bought a cell phone.

The same is happening with LED lighting. LEDs are mini light emitters. They last for 100,000 hours, are virtually indestructible, and require a fraction of the energy needed by a regular bulb to produce the same amount of light (which means they can be powered by low-wattage solar panels). Why haven't LEDs replaced lightbulbs in the U.S.? There are two reasons. First, we already have a system that works. People are slow to change unless there is a big advantage. Second, the LED bulb replacements are pricey.

The situation is different in poor villages. Villagers know the dangers of kerosene, that it is unhealthy, requires a long trip to the market, and is expensive. LED lights on the other hand are safe and simple. Hook an LED light up to a battery and a solar panel, and light appears in a thatched hut. The clincher is that a forty dollar LED system can last for decades, while kerosene costs fifty-two dollars every year.

Eventually the U.S. will switch over. Already there is a push to replace all traffic signal lights with LEDs. Another example is the incandescent bulb flashlight which is rapidly being replaced by LED flashlights. It is estimated that within the next ten years, with dropping prices, LEDs will replace lightbulbs in U.S. households. There is an advantage to accelerating this changeover.

If every household in the U.S. replaced one 60-watt light-bulb with a 2.5-watt LED bulb, we could save over 24,000 megawatts (million) per day. That's the amount of electricity produced by the Palo Verde Nuclear Generating Station in Arizona, the largest electrical generation facility in the U.S.

It took several months to come up with a rough outline for the expedition. It was a general set of goals that included adventure, charity, and education. The next step was to go from general to specific. I bought books on camels, India, the Hindi language, and solar energy. I made long to-do lists on my computer of people to contact and equipment to buy. I printed out maps and traced out the route we would follow. I enjoyed looking at the increasingly detailed itinerary. Dan did not share in this particular joy.

Dan thinks I go overboard on planning.

"I'm worried," said Dan over the phone. "I've looked at the plan you sent me. It looks like a bloomin' tour package schedule. How's it going to be an adventure if you have everything figured out to the last minute?"

I had put a lot of work into the "tour schedule" and was a little peeved at Dan's lack of enthusiasm. It was year two of the planning, and we were only weeks away from leaving for India. I took a calming breath and said, "Dan, you're concerned there won't be any spontaneity?"

Dan, who is pretty good at reading my moods, said, "Don't get me wrong, I can see you've put a lot of work into it, but it seems a bit rigid."

"Rigid," I said taking another calming breath. "You're worried about something happening like an alien spacecraft landing in the field next to us, and I'm going to say, 'Sorry, no time to stop. Alien spacecraft aren't on the schedule. We've got tickets for the Taj Mahal at 2:14.' "

Even though Dan was on the phone in England, I could imagine him pursing his lips and nodding. Of the two of us, Dan is most likely to say, "lighten up," while I'm most likely to say, "tighten up."

"Come on Dan, you know me. I'm a control freak. I don't feel comfortable unless I think through the possibilities," I paused. "But if it will make you feel better, I think the plan will fall apart. Reality will spit on it. Once we are on the road, there are too many unknowns. Think of the plan as a horoscope, a hazy outline of possibilities."

The idea that the plan would fall apart made Dan happy. "So you agree that everything is not written in stone?"

"Absolutely," I agreed.

"Brilliant," said Dan. "See you in India."

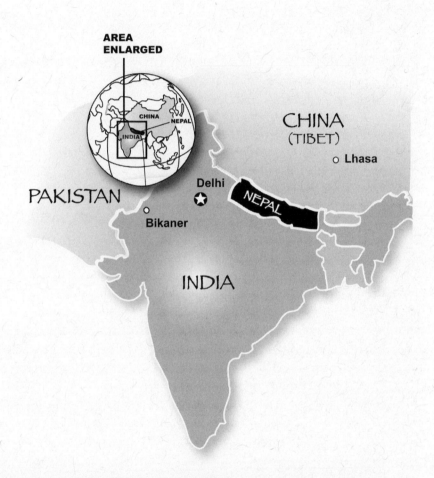

The plan was to start at Bikaner, India, near the Pakistan border and travel across India, Nepal, and China to reach Lhasa, Tibet. Little did we know that we had bitten off more than we could chew.

India Arrival

Several weeks later, at the tail end of August 2004, I touched down in India. Dan, who had arrived a few days earlier, met me at the airport. I had several hundred pounds of gear. Dan had a flower lei. He pushed his way through the thick crowd and placed the ring of blossoms around my neck.

Admiring the saffron-orange flowers, I asked, "Where are the hula girls? I thought leis were Hawaiian."

"They are also a traditional Indian welcome," explained Dan. "Let's get this lot of gear out of here before someone pinches a duffle. I've got a taxi waiting."

Part of the fun of travel is making comparisons between what you are and aren't used to. Arriving in Delhi, India, the first thing I wasn't used to was the traffic.

"Whoa, that was close," I said through clenched teeth as our taxi swerved to miss yet another vehicle. "Dan, this is all your fault."

"Why my fault?" said Dan. "I'm not driving."

"Because you're British."

"What does that have to do with the traffic?"

"It's simple. When the British Empire ruled India, they did all sorts of senseless things like beating defenseless villagers, throwing women and children down wells, and telling India what side of the road to drive on. In America we drive on the right hand side of the road. If we drive on the right side, logic says the other side is the wrong side."

Dan looked at me funny. He sometimes has trouble following my logic.

While drivers in India supposedly follow the British rule of driving on the left side of the road, there are many rebels. They think the highway is the land of the free and home of the brave. No guts, no glory. So they drive wherever it is convenient. A motorcycle, ignoring all rules of safety, roared towards us. A man was driving. His passenger, a sari-clad woman, perched sidesaddle on the back of the weaving Suzuki, her hand resting lightly on his shoulder. She was completely relaxed, one high-heeled shoe dangled precariously on the end of her toes as if she were sitting in a coffee shop. As they zoomed by, I expected to see shoe and passenger go flying into the air. High-wire circus acts show less daring than this motorcycle pair.

To take my mind off the near-death experience of riding in a taxi, I counted the number of dents on car bodies we passed. The average car had three dings per side. I didn't see an unscratched vehicle except in a dealer's showroom window.

As a teenager I studied an encyclopedic set of rules to get my drivers license: how many feet do you keep between your bumper and the car in front of you when traveling 60 mph? Who has right-of-way at a four-way signal if all cars arrive at the same time? How many seconds must your blinker be on before changing lanes? In India, the practical driving code can be simplified to three rules.

Rule one, honk. The first thing to wear out on a car in India is the horn. Indian drivers get as much joy out of honking their horns as a six-year-old gets from beating a toy drum. It's a way for a driver to say, "Look at me. I'm about to squeeze my car into a space between your car and the bumper in front of you with two inches to spare." There is no shyness about honking. Printed in big letters across the tailgates of trucks you read, "Horn Please." Even kids on bicycles ring their bells at every opportunity, as if they are preparing for the day when they can drive and honk. Somehow, in all the honk-a-thon confusion, our driver seemed to be able to tell which honks were directed at him.

Rule two, don't hit anything.

Rule three, if you do hit something, make sure it is smaller than your vehicle unless of course it is a cow, in which case you should swerve and hit another car.

This rule requires more explanation. In India, cows are holy. They are part of the Hindu religion. This divine status means that cows have equal access to the Indian road system. On the busiest city street you find cows wandering among the cars, buses, motorcycles, and rickshaws. You can reach out of your taxi window and pat a bull's butt. They ignore the honking, near misses, and congested traffic, as if they know they are watched over by the gods.

In India, cows are better protected than animals like the Northern Spotted Owl on the U.S. endangered species list. If you kill a cow, you can go to jail for six months or more. When I arrived in Delhi, this law confused me. In shops you see shoes and other items made from cow leather. I thought, "Somebody has to be killing cows." Turned out, I was wrong. When a cow dies of natural causes, the leather and bones may be used, but not the flesh. Hindus do not eat cow meat. (If a cow's treatment in India seems strange, think about dogs and cats in the U.S. Not too many Americans eat doggie steaks or fried feline. We don't even use their skins for Hush Puppy shoes or kitty fur coats).

To a foreigner, cows seem to be their own masters, but this isn't exactly true. About 80 percent of the cows are owned, and their owners are well aware of the habits of their animals. The cows are not wandering aimlessly. They are the city's garbage collectors and recyclers. They nose around among the trash thrown out in the streets, looking for vegetable scraps, paper covered in food waste, clippings from gardens—anything munchable. While this junk food diet seems unhealthy, many of the cows have sleek coats and well-muscled bodies. Squeezing by one of these giant hump-backed Brahmas on a crowded sidewalk you think, "These are the kind of bulls that stomp cowboys in rodeos." Fortunately, most of these steers are as laid back as old hippies.

After the herd has spent the day rummaging through the city's waste, their owners find and milk them. The milk is then used by the family, or sold. In the early morning men and boys balancing

Cattle in India walk down the streets and sidewalks like they own the city.

milk cans on their bicycles ride to a central processing plant in the city to sell their milk.

To supplement their "garbage" diet, these sacred cows sometimes steal fresh fruit and vegetables from vendors' stalls. I was told that the vendors must let the cattle do what they want because they are protected by the gods. That's not what I saw. Shop owners chase cattle away from their tables. In one case I saw a man whacking a cow with a stick. The animal had been chewing on the seat of his parked motorcycle. Cows crave the sweaty salt that collects on a motorcycle seat—sort of a Suzuki salt lick.

Into the Mouse's Maze

Our hotel room in Delhi, at the Rahul Palace, came complete with a marble floor, an airplane-propeller-sized ceiling fan, and one mouse. The mouse more or less kept to himself, appearing at a crack in the wall whenever we were careless and dropped a potato chip on the floor. Compared to other places we stayed in India, the Palace was expensive—thirty dollars a night. But it was in the heart of the action. The main bazaar was a rickshaw ride away.

Autorickshaws, also known as *putt-putts* because of the sound they make, consist of a motorcycle engine attached to a large three-wheeled tricycle with a roof, a windshield, and low sides. Putt-putts are the minitaxis of Indian cities. They seat two passengers comfortably and six uncomfortably. We often saw grandma perched next to the driver with mom and dad crammed in back with two kids and a baby on their laps.

Flagging down a rickshaw I asked, "How much for a ride to the main bazaar?"

He replied, "Whatever you want."

It sounded like a generous offer. Dan and I scrunched into the back seat.

I soon discovered that when a rickshaw driver said, "Whatever you want," that's not what he meant. "Whatever you want," translates to "You don't know the going rate for an autorickshaw ride in my country. What I think is expensive, you, a wealthy foreigner, might think is cheap. So, being inexperienced, you will pay me more than I could get from a local."

When the rickshaw driver pulled over at the entrance to the bazaar, I paid the driver a sum that an Indian would pay for a ride. The driver looked insulted. "It is not enough," he said.

I replied, "You said pay whatever you want."

He retorted, "This won't pay for my gas." He was trying to make me feel cheap. He succeeded. To avoid the hassle of haggling, I ended up paying three times as much as his regular fare—about two dollars.

Later, I learned the best response to "Whatever you want." First, I'd offer a reasonable price. If the driver nodded, I'd jot the price down into a pocket notebook, holding it up for the driver to see. This was a good reason for carrying a notebook. It seems that putt-putting around in traffic fumes all day leaves drivers with bad memories. At the end of a trip, when I would count the agreed number of rupees into a driver's hand, some would shake their heads. "Not enough."

"Yes it is. That's what we agreed upon, 50 rupees."

"No, it was more, 150 rupees."

Then I'd whip out my notebook like a trial lawyer. "Here's the price we agreed on." It's amazing how a little printed number made things go so much smoother.

Standing at the edge of the main bazaar, India's original mall, we teetered on the edge of chaos. Dense throngs of people, shop signs in Hindi script, subterranean odors, a commotion of motion. I felt a rat's tail of caution tickle the back of my neck. Part of me wanted to explore, but another part of me wanted to retreat to the safe confines of our hotel room and flip through a guidebook. Acquaintances often think I'm a big risk taker—close friends know better. My wife will be the first to tell you I'm risk-averse. If everything is worked out and I know the odds are in my favor, I'll plunge in. When there are lots of unknowns, I've got chicken blood. Thankfully, I'm 6' 4" and my exploring buddy, Dan, weighs in at 230–240 lbs. His weight depends on how many potato chips he's eaten lately. We figure bad guys would think twice before jumping us. This is also a good reason to keep moving—it gives people with bad intentions less time to calculate the odds.

Dropping from an airplane into a foreign country should make you cautious. That's because your safety alert system doesn't work properly. Unless you are fluent in the local language, you no longer understand people—you may as well be deaf. Someone could say, "I think I will bash you on the head and steal your camera" right to your face in a foreign language and you stand there nodding politely. Then, when you do get into trouble, you discover that you are mute, unable to ask for help because you don't know the language. Fortunately, you can still see. That's why I acted like a lighthouse, periodically pivoting or looking over my shoulder to check what was going on around me.

As we entered the main bazaar, I thought, *The mouse back at our hotel designed this place.* The bazaar was a maze of nooks, crannies, and cubbyholes. In places half the size of my garage, families

The main bazaar in Delhi is a busy place. Workshops, storefronts, and living spaces are all crammed together.

combined their living space with a workshop and a storefront. Following the serpentine alleys I passed: a blacksmith pounding out a replacement car part on an anvil, a merchant surrounded by colorful spices, an old woman stringing flowers, a goldsmith flaming a piece of jewelry, and the butchers.

The butchers occupied their own section in the maze. Their area was enough to make you a vegetarian. I passed a man using a cleaver to make four rapid cuts in the ankle of some livestock to remove the hoof. Shanks, shoulders, and flanks were slapped onto meat hooks at the front of the shop. Flies swarmed over the unprotected meat. A dump truck jammed into a dark alley overflowed with the bloodied remains of a barnyard-worth of animals. I sidled past the truck, hopscotching over pools of blood and swatting at flies. A butcher, seeing my discomfort, held out a decapitated goat's head with blue horns. I shook my head and picked up my pace as he called after me.

In the tight narrow alleys, sunlight was scarce. Rounding a corner, I was attracted to a bright spot in the shadows. A fire crackled under a battered copper cauldron. A man leaned over the cooking pot with a ladle the size of a canoe paddle. As he stirred, his sweat dripped into the pot.

What keeps all these little shops going is the rupee. The rupee is the currency of India.

Black Market

"Dan, I was told American dollars are worthless in the desert. People won't sell us camels for U.S. money. We need to exchange dollars for Indian money, rupees. We need to make a trip to the bank."

Dan got a sly look on his face, "You want to try something more interesting than a bank?"

"What?" I asked cautiously.

"I've been talking to the person at the front desk of the hotel. He knows a guy who will give us more rupees per dollar than the bank will give us."

"What you're talking about is the black market. Guys who can get you anything for the right price."

Dan nodded, "You said you wanted to make our sponsor money go as far as possible."

"We could also get swindled, counterfeit bills, or robbed at gun point," I said.

"What if I make the arrangements? No dark alley. The exchanger comes to our hotel room. We're both big guys. You're a black belt in karate. What do you say?"

It did sound more interesting than standing in a line at the bank. "Set it up."

Thirty minutes later there was a knock at the door.

"Come in."

We expected a heavy-set person wearing a dark suit, carrying a briefcase, with a bodyguard or two. Instead, a scrawny little man carrying a grocery bag sidled into our room. Dan shut the door, locked it, and leaned against the frame. The exchanger looked at Dan nervously. Apparently, getting ripped off can go both ways. The little guy was more worried about us than we were about him.

I laid $2,300 in American bills on the table. Twenty-three hundred dollars is more money than many people in India earn in ten years. Our money exchanger thumbed through the stack, holding each bill up to the light, checking for counterfeits. When he was done, he pulled fat packets of rupees from his paper bag. Apparently, paper bags attract less attention on the street than briefcases. At 46 rupees to the dollar, he pulled out over 100,000 rupees. As he had done, I held each bill up to the light checking for counterfeits. There's a thin metallic strip woven into Indian money that indicates it is good. It took me thirty minutes to go through hundreds of bills.

There was a knock at the door. Dan, the money exchanger, and I tensed.

"Room service," said the voice on the other side of the door.

We hadn't ordered room service.

Dan checked the door lock and said, "Go away."

Ten minutes later we let the black market money exchanger out of the room. We stared at the ransom-sized pile of rupees on the table.

"How are we going to carry so much cash?" asked Dan. "It won't fit in a money belt around the waist. We'd each look pregnant."

I thought about it for a moment and said, "Hand me those bags of potato chips."

Carefully slitting the seams of the bags, I dumped the chips into a bowl, which Dan immediately started eating. "Give me a couple of packets of rupees," I said. I slid the rupees into the potato chip bag while talking, "If a thief starts rifling through our gear he might just assume we're junk food addicts and ignore the bags." I carefully resealed the bag. "I've also brought a money belt. We stick a small amount of cash into the belt along with some fake credit cards (I'd brought some old expired cards from home). Thieves know that foreigners carry credit cards, so the fake cards make the belt look like the real thing. Now I put the money belt in an obvious hiding place. Then we hope any robber grabs the belt rather than the potato chip bags."

"The potato chip bag vault. Brilliant!" said Dan, "Unless of course, we get a hungry thief."

Dan counts through our stacks of rupees. The big Gurkha knife next to the money was a security precaution.

We were ready to travel.

Dan and I headed to the train station to buy tickets. Walking through Delhi, I saw bird's nests of electrical wires. We're not talking an organized weaver bird nest, more like a cuckoo bird. Wire tangles hung from the sides of buildings, dangled over roadways, and protruded from open boxes. In a rupee-tight economy, these wire jumbles are signs that shout, "If it works—keep using it." This popular philosophy was embraced by the Delhi train station.

We had two ticket-buying choices. We could enter an unruly line of shoving people who looked like they were trying to get out of a burning movie theatre or we could go to the second floor of the train station, which is reserved for tourists. On the second floor there was no pushing or shoving. We sat on old couches. For entertainment we stared at faded upholstery, faded walls, and faded posters that advertised "The Fairy Train" or an equally stirring photo of the "transport building of 1950." The ticket agents sat in front of thick ledgers, similar to the ones used by Scrooge and Bob Cratchit, and recorded all critical information for ticket issuance in longhand. There was not a computer in sight. It took an average of ten to fifteen minutes to fill out each ticket. If you like math, you could count the number of customers sitting on the faded couches in front of you. Four ticket buyers equaled a forty to sixty minute wait. Double that number to eight customers and the wait increased to more than two hours due to the periodic tea breaks for agents. If there were more than eight customers, we figured we should start walking towards our destination—we would get there faster. To bond with my agent, I struck up a lively conversation. "How long have you had this job?"

Agent: "Thirty-one years."

I concluded that he would live to be 200 as he allowed absolutely nothing to hurry him or add stress to his life.

We booked a night train out of Delhi. Our first-class sleeper cabin had bunks and a fan. A fan was mandatory in the humid heat. The bathroom was just down the corridor. The little stall had two footprints outlined around a hole in the floor. You made deposits directly on to the tracks. The first few miles out of the train station were particularly fragrant. We click-clacked out of the fumey station towards the desert town of Bikaner.

We took a train from Delhi to Bikaner in the Thar Desert.

On the Edge of the Thar Desert

Bikaner is located in the state of Rajasthan, India, not far from the Pakistan border. The city is surrounded by the Thar Desert, the seventh largest sandbox in the world: 92,000 square miles. That's enough dunes, rocks, and scrub vegetation to cover the states of New York, Vermont, Massachusetts, New Hampshire, Rhode Island, Delaware, and Connecticut combined. Bikaner was once a fortress town along a camel caravan route ruled by the local maharaja.

We chose Bikaner because of the Internet. When I typed "camels India," I came up with The National Research Center on Camels in Bikaner. The center boasts that it is one of the top camel research centers in the world. Of course there aren't a lot of camel research centers.

As part of my trip planning, I put together a list of researchers working at the center and emailed them. Most of my emails went unanswered. Then I got a hit. A Dr. Mehta was intrigued by our expedition. He agreed to advise us. So Bikaner it was.

Beware of Trout

As the train pulled into Bikaner, so did our 'karma'. Karma is big in the Hindu religion, a faith practiced by many Indians. It's a religious version of cause and effect. Simply stated, if you plant a papaya seed, you get papayas. Plant poison oak and you get a rash. In other words, good comes to those who do good, and bad comes to those who do bad. Dan was convinced that the wonderful coincidences that were about to become part of our trip were karma.

"We are doing a good thing," said Dan. "So we can expect good stuff to happen to us. What goes around comes around."

As we carried our duffel bags off the train, I prepared for another kind of cause and effect. I was ready for the dreaded tout. The first time I saw the word in a guidebook, I misread it. I thought it said trout. So I read the phrase in my guide book as, "Beware of trout that swarm around airline, bus, and train terminals looking for tourists." Actually, touts are annoyingly pushy salespeople who target tourists. In a way, touts are like trout. Drop a juicy tourist into their midst and they go into a feeding frenzy. They cluster around you, nibbling at your sleeves, sometimes boldly tugging you in their preferred direction. These touts are fishing, trying to get you to bite their line. They say things like, "Taxi?" "I will be your guide." "Come, I have a hotel." "Do you need a bus ticket?" "Where are you from? You must come to my house for tea, my brother's shop has the most amazing souvenirs." Often they won't take no for an answer—at least not an English no.

In Delhi I discovered how to scatter touts. It was as effective as using garlic and crosses to repel vampires. When a tout approached and insisted I follow, buy, or listen to him, I shook my head in the negative. Of course he ignored me. That's when I pulled away, and said, *Hindi aatii hay?* (Do you speak Hindi?) This was a surprise coming from a foreigner. They invariably nodded yes. Then in clear Hindi I said *nahii!* (no). Speaking Hindi suggests you aren't the average dazed and helpless tourist. They realized they were wasting their time and went looking for easier prey.

The Bikaner train platform wasn't swarming, teeming, or spilling over with touts. There was only one. As he approached I prepared my most forceful Hindi *no!* Before I said anything, he simply handed me a business card. That was a surprise. No long-winded sales pitch. A glance at the card showed the name of a hotel, Harasar Haveli. This was the same hotel I had circled in my guidebook. What a coincidence. One tout and he just happened to be from the hotel we had chosen months before. Then he mentioned that he had a brand new SUV waiting to take us to the hotel. Considering our mountain of luggage, this was a real piece of luck. In Hindi I said *jii* (yes).

The SUV driver was an unusually tall Indian with jet-black hair and a hint of a smile.

As we piled our gear into his SUV he asked in fluent English, "Where are you from?"

"Jim's a Yank and I'm British," replied Dan.

"You have a lot of luggage," said the driver. "Is this your first trip to India?"

"I traveled across India and Kashmir several years ago after working in Nepal," said Dan. "All the gear is for our expedition." Dan paused for dramatic effect. "We are going to buy camels and ride across India."

The driver hesitated, "Across India. Interesting. I was in contact with someone last year who had a similar plan."

I thought *Oh, no. Copycat adventurers. We won't be the first.* Out loud, I asked, "Did they show up?"

"No," said the driver.

I sighed with relief, thinking, *Your average Indiana Jones wannabes, but in reality a bunch of adventure wusses.*

"I was in contact with this person over the Internet," said the driver. "I think he was from California. He was setting up an expedition to ride across India to Nepal and then into Tibet, if I remember correctly."

"Whoa. That's our plan, and I'm from California," I said. This was too weird.

Our driver continued, "He asked a lot of questions. How far can camels travel in a day? What do they eat? Did I know a veterinarian?"

"Wait a minute," I said. "Those are the kinds of questions I was asking before the trip. What's your name?"

"My name is Visvajeet, but call me Bubbles. It's easier to pronounce."

"Bubbles? I don't know a Bubbles."

"Bubbles Singh."

"Singh," I said. "I was in contact with a Singh at the beginning of our Internet search."

I remembered the emails. Early on, I'd contacted an Indian tour company, Club Travels and Holiday Adventures. One of the agents, Rajen Singla, said he'd help me locate a source for buying camels. He put me in touch with a Birendra Singh. I began to see the connection. Families in India are extensive. If you know one Singh, you are automatically in contact with a network of Singhs. I guessed that my requests for information were passed along to family members who might have the answers. My requests must have trickled down to Bubbles Singh, who was now sitting next to me. What a coincidence.

When it became apparent that we had been introduced over the Internet a year before, Bubbles bubbled over with enthusiasm. We had actually made it to Bikaner. He thought the project had been abandoned and that was why we hadn't continued our email correspondence.

"I am very interested in your expedition," said Bubbles. "My staff and I will do anything we can to help."

"Your staff?" I said puzzled.

"Yes, I own the hotel you will be staying at."

We were to discover that Bubbles was full of surprises.

His hotel, the Harasar Haveli, is on the outskirts of Bikaner. It is a multistoried structure, which is good in a hot desert environment. Being even twelve inches above the ground can lower the temperature by thirty degrees. If you think height isn't important because you have air conditioning, think again. If one thing is reliable in Bikaner, it is blackouts. The electricity is guaranteed to shut down once a day if not more; so much for air conditioning. We moved into a room on the third floor. For about twenty dollars a night we got a freshly painted high-ceilinged room, a polished marble floor, a clean bathroom, air conditioning, a fan, a TV, and access to a rooftop restaurant that looks out over the city. The Harasar became our base of operations.

After dumping our gear, we went looking for an autorickshaw driver to introduce us to Bikaner.

Bikaner radiates from the red sandstone walls of Jungaragh
Fort, once the stronghold of Maharajah Singh, now a museum.
Remnants of fortress walls weave through the city. Older parts of
town are a bewildering maze of narrow, twisting streets, dead ends,
and densely packed buildings. A homing pigeon would get lost
here. The city's layout only makes sense when you look at it

One of the palace buildings in Jungaragh Fort.

through old eyes. In the book *The Camel and the Wheel*, Richard Bulliet explains the logic behind town planning. At a time when desert bandits dreamed of becoming respectable Maharajas, planners knew that square blocks and parallel streets allowed an enemy to gallop into town in a lightning attack. Straight streets wouldn't give the townspeople enough time to mount a defense. A muddle of serpentine streets slowed and confused attackers. Today it has the same effect on tourists.

Narrow streets also make sense in this environment. In Europe and the West, the introduction of wagons and carts meant that streets had to be wide enough for two wagons to pass. Desert towns, like Bikaner, relied on pack camels for transport. This meant that streets only needed to be wide enough for two camels to pass. These narrow winding streets also helped to bottleneck attackers, diminish sandstorm winds, and provide much needed shade in a hot environment.

Bag-o'-guts

During one of our visits around town, Bubbles suggested we visit a local meat market, not for the meat, but for the show. While I worked on a piece of equipment, Bubbles briefed Dan on what to ask the butchers.

As we parked our autorickshaw next to the meat market, I said, "That's a lot of dogs." A pack of twenty mongrels surrounded the market. I was hesitant to get out.

Dan eyed them warily, "You know we talked about getting a dog to take on the trip. I don't think anyone would miss one of these mutts."

"Which one were you thinking of?" I nodded, "The one lying in the sewage, three-legged blackie over there, or look, one who's lost his hair to mange? He'd stay cool in the desert." I shook my head, "Now I know why I got rabies shots."

Dan agreed, "Yeah, they are a nasty looking lot."

"I wonder why there are so many of them?"

We soon found out.

Walking into a dark cavern of a building, I ignored the live chickens held out to us, the blind stares of severed sheep heads, and the chop-snip-whack-hack of busy knives on flesh.

Stopping at the nearest vendor, Dan said, "We'd like some guts." The butcher did a little chop-snip, and for a few rupees, Dan got what he asked for.

Stepping back outside with his bag-o'-guts, Dan said, "Here goes." He reached into the bag snagging a piece of kidney and flung it into the air. It soared upward and came back down with a splat next to Dan's foot. Our doggie audience perked up. One came over, sniffed, and cleaned up.

Dan tossed another piece of meat skyward.

Swish. A meat hawk snagged the chunk in midair. In moments the ground was criss-crossed by the shadows of alert raptors. This was like feeding pigeons popcorn, only these birds were big enough to eat pigeons. These are the meat hawks of Bikaner. They hang out around this particular butcher shop to entertain tourists. Dan added to the entertainment. Especially when he'd toss some offal skyward, the bird would miss, and the guts would come back down on Dan's head. It takes a certain degree of skill to time your throw with the swoop of a hawk. Any misses become doggie dinners. Our canine audience appreciated that Dan missed half of his hawk throws.

After feeding the meat hawks we arranged to meet Dr. Mehta, our camel advisor.

"Everything is a learning experience."

Dr. Mehta's office was located at the Bikaner camel research station on the outskirts of town. A fence encircled a number of clean, well-kept buildings. The gardening was simple and neat. We checked in with the guard at the gate and were escorted to Dr. Mehta's office.

The motivational speaker Anthony Robbins says, "There is no such thing as failure, everything is a learning experience." Dr. Mehta was to be a learning experience.

At this point, my only contact with Dr. Mehta had been through the Internet and email. In our email correspondence he informed me that he had written such papers as *Genetic differentiation of*

Indian camel breeds (Camelus dromedaries) using random oligo-nucleotide primers. Hindsight suggests we would have been better off with someone who had written *How to Ride a Camel.* But then, I have a weakness. I believe that anyone who has a Ph.D. behind their name is an expert. Next time I will pick someone with a P.E. degree—doctorate in Practical Experience.

In our emails, Dr. Mehta let it be known that he wasn't interested in being part of our project unless we relied solely on his recommendations. At one point he withdrew his offer of help when I mentioned I was contacting a veterinarian in Bikaner. This was one of the reasons I stopped my correspondence with Bubbles Singh. Dr. Mehta wanted no competition. I figured that Dr. Mehta had access to a whole herd of camels and all the experience that went with it. I thought he would be our best resource. Though I was puzzled why he didn't want us to work with other advisors.

As Dan and I entered Dr. Mehta's office, I noticed that everything on his desk—pencils, papers, and calendar—was laid out precisely. Even the paper he put down as we entered was angled just so. A huge swamp cooler occupied a fifth of his office.

Dan and I squeezed in next to the swamp cooler and accepted his offer of tea. As we talked I knew we were in trouble. He spoke English, but I only understood one out of every three words. "It's _____ _____ pick," Mehta said, "_____ _____or____ _____ aggressive _____ _____ kill _____ _____ foreigner."

I replied, "Really?"

Later we learned that the best English speakers speak "tourist English." These are Indians with no formal training who pick up their English on the streets. They understand that you only make money from tourists if the tourist understands you. Academics need not worry about being understood when they speak English.

Still, I thought we were OK. Dan kept nodding his head and saying "Really?" I figured Dan would fill me in later. After all Dan is British and constantly reminded me that Brits invented the English language. Later I discovered that Dan understood about two out of every three words. We pooled our impressions to piece together what the doctor had said.

As we got to know each other, Dr. Mehta talked about a stack of scientific papers he'd written on the genetic differences between camels. He could tell you intimate differences between Bikaneri, Jasalimeri, and Karachi camel breeds. And yet he was not fond of camels.

"Sheep are my real passion," said Dr. Mehta. "But higher-ups determine where we conduct research, and camels won out over sheep."

"You should just get crazy and go with the sheep," I suggested. But he shook his head, resigned to the power of higher-ups.

"Would you like to see our herd?" asked Dr. Mehta. "They should be coming in for feeding."

In the field behind the research station we saw a string of camels being driven in by a camel rider. Even with my limited experience, I could tell these were healthy animals. They were sleek coated muscular animals with bright eyes and plump humps. Part of the research done at the station is to produce a superior breed of camel for domestic use. Camels in Rajasthan are used for plowing fields, transportation, pulling carts, and milk production.

I asked, "Will we be able to buy four camels from the research station?"

"No," replied Dr. Mehta. "Our camels are chosen for specific experiments and breeding. We will find a herder who has camels for sale."

When we asked Dr. Mehta to pose with one of the research station camels, he stood a safe distance from the tethered animal. In all the time we spent with Dr. Mehta, I never saw him touch a camel. We also learned that he did not ride camels. This is not uncommon in a country where the educated try to distance themselves from the common farmer. I would anticipate a similar response in the U.S. if I were to ask a homeowner if they enjoyed pumping their own septic tank. Why would anyone willingly do that?

At about this time, a number of red flag warnings popped up concerning my choice of an advisor. But I was so excited just being around the camels that I ignored the signs. Dr. Mehta suggested we go back to his office to make plans for visiting camel herders in the Thar Desert.

Into the Restricted Area

Several days later, we hired a four-wheel-drive jeep to take us into the desert to search for a camel seller. Into this smallish vehicle, a driver, Dr. Mehta, a village headsman, a veterinarian, several Raika tribesman, Dan, and I were crammed. This made the jeep's springs as useful as hood ornaments. As the jeep merrily slammed into pot-holes, swerving wildly along the track to avoid being mired in sand, Dan and I joked about the safety value of overcrowding in a seat belt-less vehicle with tires balder than my father-in-law's head.

Locating a camel herd in the Thar Desert is like the eliminating process in the game of Clue. You travel around the board, in this case the Thar Desert, checking off one location after another. No camels in this village. The goat herder hasn't seen any camels. No camel tracks visible from the road. No camels at this watering hole. The bombing range is active so they probably aren't there. Bombing range? We discovered we were in a restricted military area. We heard muffled *whooomphhs* of exploding artillery shells on a ridge several kilometers away. Supposedly, military personnel with ties to local villages inform relatives when bombing ranges will be inac-tive. During these lulls, villagers hustle in their livestock in search of fodder while the military turns a blind eye to their presence.

For several days, we drove through the restricted area. Our village guide kept us out of the active bombing area. Thorny acacia trees dotted the dryness. Dust blew in the open jeep, mixing with our sweat. Dan was tail gunner, the worst seat. He looked like he'd been basted with dirty flour and was ready for the oven. As we headed towards a popular watering hole, we slowed to pass camel carts pulling massive loads of firewood; some haul as much as 2,000 pounds. We stopped for herds of sheep, their butts dyed red, yellow, and blue. The colors distinguish one herder's animals from another's. Flying beetles the size of fifty-cent pieces smacked into our radiator grill. When they weren't smacking, they were snacking. Their preferred meal is poop. Like circus performers on balance balls, they rolled dung balls towards a hole-studded embankment, dung beetle city. By now, Dan, covered in dust, looked like a dung ball. The local tribesmen stared as we passed. We were an unusual sight in this area.

In some villages we stopped to shop for camels. This was like two Amish farmers trying to buy a piece of property in Manhattan from the king of real estate, Donald Trump. As the Trumps of Humps, camel sellers detected our inexperience. We had been warned to watch out for certain things. We might be offered camels whose humps had been pumped with air (big humps are a sign of health). Then there's the old drugged camel trick. That mellow camel you bought yesterday now wants to wrestle with you. This is a real danger—an aggressive camel hooks you with its neck and slams you to the ground. Then he pretends to be a rolling pin, and you are the pie crust. With the enthusiasm of ignorance, we thumped hocks, humps, and rumps. Of course we had our camel advisor and a veterinarian, but Dan and I were surprisingly savvy. We could tell when a camel was missing a leg or looked like it had been in a fight with a garbage truck. Most of the camels were obvious rejects.

It took several days to locate a camel herd with the features we wanted. We were looking for females, four to six years of age, not pregnant, in good health, and trained to ride. We wanted females because males would enter rut during the course of the trip. Rut is a condition in which male camels go from being reasonable Dr. Jekylls to aggressive and dangerous Mr. Hydes for several months out of every year. The herd we found in the desert had over fifty animals, many of them females.

While the herders separated out a group of camels, we were invited to sit on goat hair blankets in the shade of a spindly acacia tree. The herder's few possessions—blankets, a pan, several cups, water bottles, and a bag of food—lay on a ridge overlooking a small valley where the camels were feeding. In addition to the camels, the tribesmen were baby-sitting a group of lambs. The bleating newborns were tethered around the campsite. They looked like the stuffed Lambie I'd had as a child. One herder collected twigs to start a fire. It was classic. It was also something I dreaded. We were about to be offered tea.

Raika tribesman in the Thar Desert with camels in the background.

"If you do not share tea with the herders," advised Dr. Mehta, "they will be offended. Drinking tea is a polite respectful custom."

Not accepting this hospitality would be rude and might mess up any deal we hoped to make. I didn't want to look like an ill-mannered, disrespectful foreigner. I also didn't want to mess up my stomach. Foreigners have to be careful about what they eat and drink. I watched as the herder cleaned teacups with sand mixed with fresh lamb droppings. Another herder kneaded a camel's teats, squirt-squirt, out came camel milk. The tea-maker picked his nose thoughtfully as he mixed the tea leaves, sugar, and camel milk into boiling water. Lamb droppings, unpasteurized camel's milk, and boogers …. *Great*, I thought. *Play Bacteria Lotto with chances to win hoof and mouth disease, Salmonella, and the booger surprise.* I accepted the tea. At least they had boiled the water and milk. That would probably kill a lot of bacteria, right? I brought the scalding liquid to the rim of the teacup. I held it there as long as I could, hoping to destroy any biohazards on the lip-touching part of the cup. The herders watched expectantly. I sipped. Mmmmmm, it was delicious, must have been the camel's milk, or maybe the lamb droppings? By the time I finished my tea, they had collected the camels for us to look at.

A Raika tribesman held one of the camels. I passed my hands over the animal's rump, kneading and feeling the muscles and bones. I had no idea of what I was doing. As a potential buyer I thought I should look knowledgeable. At the very least I would be able to tell if a bone was sticking out or an eye was missing.

Four camels met our criteria. We asked to see them ridden. The Raika herder grabbed a camel's neck and swung aboard the hump. He was as good as any American bronco rider and skillfully maneuvered three of the camels around the desert with only a rope halter, a blanket for a saddle, and a switch pulled from a bush. For some reason he did not ride the fourth camel and simply pointed it out in the herd. He slyly explained, "The camels are all the same. There is no reason to ride the fourth camel. Now we should talk price." His first price and conditions were high and unacceptable. We tried bargaining, but he wouldn't budge. I shook my head and explained, through Dr. Mehta who was interpreting for us, that we would find another camel seller.

We walked away from the deal. Just before leaving in the jeep, a boy scurried after us with a message. The camel seller would change the conditions and the cost.

Dan and I talked it over.

"I don't think Dr. Mehta is too enthusiastic about coming back out in the desert with us," I said. "I think he'd rather be back at his lab."

Dan nodded, "Finding the camels isn't easy."

"Yeah," I agreed. "But something bothers me about that fourth camel."

"Let's ask them to ride it," said Dan.

When we approached the Raika and told him we wanted to see the fourth camel up close and being ridden, he repeated that it wasn't necessary. We insisted he ride it or no deal.

To catch the fourth camel, the tribesman rounded up forty camels. They held a long rope and made a big circle around the animals. Each herder was like a post in a corral. Then they slowly decreased the size of the circle. One by one, camels were released from the rope corral until the one we wanted was the only one left. Dan and I looked at each other. Nothing like this had been necessary to catch the other camels we looked at. And it only got more interesting. The herders showed a lot of respect to the fourth camel, jumping back when she wheeled on them. Using ropes, they forced her to the ground. Both her front and hind legs were hobbled. The boy tying the ropes was very cautious. As he slid the ropes into place, the camel voiced her displeasure with a 747 roar. A halter and blanket saddle were affixed to her back. The herder asked, "Would you like to ride this camel?" Everything I'd seen this far screamed no! I shook my head. The Raika then got on. His riding method was completely different from the previous camels. He mounted at the very back of the animal rather than up by the neck. When the hobbles were released, the camel sling-shoted into a gallop, its rider clinging to the hump. After dashing through bushes, under trees, and over dunes in an impressive display of a camel ignoring all attempts to be steered, the herder ejected from the running animal like a test pilot. When the Raika got back to us, he was sweating and breathing hard. The camel seemed to have enjoyed the whole affair a lot more than he did. Then the Raika looked us straight in the eye and without hesitation said, "She needs a little work." Dan and I almost fell down we were laughing so hard.

Then a strange thing happened. As I watched the camel, there seemed to be such intelligence in the animal's eyes and such spirit that I immediately liked her. Of course, this kind of bonding only happens in Disney movies. Wild crazed camels don't bond after looking into your eyes. They are more likely to stomp you until your eyes pop out of your head. After more haggling, we made arrangements for all four camels to be delivered to the camel research station at Bikaner. The camel seller promised that he would help us train the fourth camel.

Leaving the desert, we ran out of gas. Fortunately we were close to a village. The villagers brought out their beds for us to sit on. The beds are simple square wooden frames with strips of cloth woven over the framework, like a lawn chair, to make the mattress. While we waited, someone went in search of a gas station. Soon there was a crowd of curious villagers. Dan opened the evening's entertainment by singing a song from *My Fair Lady*. Then he organized the villagers and soon had them singing, "The rain in Spain stays mainly in the plain…" Even though they didn't speak English, they were surprisingly good, picking up both the tune and the pronunciation. At intermission, I shared a mini slide show of the day's events, scrolling though scenes on my digital camera. The audience jostled for position. Pictures of the water hole were a big hit as were images of relatives and neighbors. Eventually the gas station arrived, a fifty-five gallon drum of gas was rolled up next to the jeep.

While waiting, one of our bald tires went flat. I helped the driver replace it with a spare that didn't look much better.

"What happens if we blow another tire?" I asked.

"That would not be good," replied the driver. "Someone would have to take the tire to be repaired."

I looked out at the dark desert night thinking it could be a long walk.

Later as we were tearing along the sand track I suggested, "Why so fast, maybe with these tires we'd be better off slowing down?"

"No, sir," said the driver. "The sooner we get back to the main road, the better. If a tire blows, it may still be early enough for us to get help fixing it."

Buyer's Remorse

Back at the hotel, guests asked us what we'd been up to. We casually replied, "Oh, buying a few camels." Like a teenager who has just bought his first car, we were stoked. Our host, Bubbles, did not share our enthusiasm.

"Controlling a rough desert camel will not be easy," he said. "The Raika herders you dealt with were born on camels. They may be able to tame a camel in two days to ride, but I wouldn't want to be the rider. Have you ridden a lot?"

"I've ridden camels for six or seven days, but I used to ride horses when I was a teen," I added hopefully. "Dan's ridden once or twice."

"Are the camels nose pegged or did they use halters?" asked Bubbles.

"Halters."

He shook his head. "Buying a camel without a nose peg is like buying a car without a steering wheel."

Bubbles had a point. I'd only ridden camels that had a wooden peg punched through one nostril. This peg is attached to a rein that is used to steer the camel. Bits, like you find on a horse, won't work on camels because they are cud-chewing animals and the bit gets in the way. The only other option, a halter, is more iffy on a stubborn animal. But maybe Bubbles was being overly cautious. He hadn't seen Hollywood movies where wild horses, killer whales, and almost rabid dogs are tamed with love and affection—usually by a ten-year-old child. His recommendation was simple.

"Get out of the deal," said Bubbles. "I'll help you find more suitable camels."

Back in our room, Dan and I had buyer's remorse. Buyer's remorse occurs when you buy something and start worrying that it was a dumb decision. We cursed Disney movies for deluding us. "We've been hasty." "Training a camel to ride in two days did seem optimistic." "Camel four was a bit wild."

The camels were to be delivered to the Bikaner Camel Research station in two days. Dan and I prayed for a sand storm, deluge, or plague of locusts to delay the delivery.

In the meantime, Bubbles offered to make inquiries as to where we might buy camels.

"Bubbles, we have a problem," I said. "Dan and I gave our word that we would buy the camels upon delivery. We are big on keeping our word."

Dan added, "It is a bind, you see. Do we go with honorable and do a ruddy stupid thing, buy the camels? Or do we go with dishonorable but smart, and back out of the deal?"

"I see," said Bubbles, "I have a suggestion. When the Raika make the delivery, give them 2,000 rupees per camel to cancel the purchase. That's about $40 per animal. They may not act happy, but it is a good deal for them. That's more than they could make in a month."

What a great idea. And as we were to learn, Bubbles had a knack for smoothing things out like a true diplomat.

It's strange how you can want something so much, and then when it is about to happen you want out. We waited for the dreaded call from Dr. Mehta telling us that the camels had arrived. It turned out that we worried for no reason. Dr. Mehta never called. In fact we had to call him—several times. As the deadline approached, we held our breath. When a full extra day passed, we felt the exhilaration of a contract lawyer who has discovered a loophole. The Raika never turned up with the camels. Dr. Mehta had no idea why, but suggested that the fourth camel, the one with spirit, had proved so difficult that the Raika had decided they wouldn't be able to train it in the agreed-upon time frame and had canceled the deal on their own. I smugly said to Dan, "I told you I liked that fourth camel."

We never found out what happened to the herders. Maybe they are still chasing Camel Four across the desert. At this point, Dr. Mehta became very busy. The Raika herder he had suggested to help us also became unavailable. They say you shouldn't change camels in midstream, but our camel sank. We switched our allegiance from Dr. Mehta to Bubbles.

Bubbles had originally refrained from getting between us and Dr. Mehta. He didn't want to upset the relationship we had with the research laboratory. As soon as Dr. Mehta withdrew his support, Bubbles leaped in.

"I want very much to help," said Bubbles. "If I could ride with you, I would. But my business keeps me here, so helping is the second best way for me to be part of your adventure. I've asked Pane Singh, he's retired military and well-respected in the villages, to accompany you in your search for camels."

All Dan and I could say was, "Thank you!"

"My advice is that you look for camels in a village," suggested Bubbles. "These camels are more likely to be trained than camels from a herd in the desert. I will go with you when I can."

Dan and I were ready to go right then.

"I think it would be best to go later in the day," said Bubbles. "These are working camels. They will be in the fields or on the road during the day. Around five o'clock, people and animals return home. We will see more camels in the village than if we go hunting for them."

It was good advice.

Again we rented a jeep and started visiting villages. Pane Singh introduced us to the families and put out the word that camel buyers were in the area. A friend of Bubbles, Ranveer Singh, gave us a good piece of advice. "Test-drive the camels before you buy." Having seen what Camel Four could do to a Raika tribesman, we were cautious. We always asked the owner to ride first. After the owner rode, Dan and I drew straws to see who would test-drive the camel. Just because the camel had behaved for the owner didn't mean the animal would obey us.

To keep track of the animals we looked at, I wrote down owners' names, their village, and made-up names for the camels. Unlike Westerners, who name every creature they own—including dogs, cats, guinea pigs, hamsters, and goldfish—Indian villagers don't name their animals. We gave the camels descriptive names like Thunder Thighs, Trojan Horse, Saddle Sore, and Psycho. We also jotted notes next to each camel's name: "had to be hit in head to be controlled by owner," "is calm standing in a crowd," "accepts food from our hands and leaves all the fingers." We took digital photos of the animals which were a good memory jog. Late in the evening, Dan and I scanned our notes and two-inch digital screens, and discussed the fine points of each animal. We were becoming camel connoisseurs.

Dan test-drives a camel. This was always a little scary because you never knew if the camel would be mild or wild.

To make our camel search go more smoothly, Dan and I used magic. Many villagers were shy, especially the children who would run away from us, two foreigners. That's when Dan or I would sit in the sand to appear less threatening. One of us would casually show an empty hand, reach up, and pluck a coin from the air. The kids, watching from a distance, edged closer. When the coin disappeared, a silk handkerchief appeared in its place. The kids moved closer. By the time we were pulling ropes through our necks, we were surrounded by children and adults. Within ten minutes we had crowds of twenty to a hundred villagers assembled for our impromptu magic shows. David Copperfield or Houdini could not have asked for more responsive audiences. Kids and adults would ask us to repeat tricks over and over. Magic was a great way to get everyone to relax around us.

Believe It or Not

Between camel-shopping trips, Ranveer Singh, Bubbles' friend, invited us for a visit. He owned Heritage Resort Hotel on the outskirts of Bikaner. As we passed through the gates, a mustachioed attendant, royally jacketed and turbaned, greeted us at the entrance. Ranveer met us in the hotel's elegant foyer of polished marble and led us out to the pool deck, where a table was set up for dinner. Candles flickered in their holders. Two waiters, in suits that looked like the tuxedo I had rented for my senior prom, started serving an eight-course Indian meal of vegetables, spicy mutton, traditional breads, and ice-cold lime juice. While enjoying the food, Ranveer entertained us with an Indian version of *Ripley's Believe It or Not*.

"There are many amazing stories in India," said Ranveer. "There is one of a lady who lived fifty years eating only a leaf a day. There were people who didn't believe her story, so doctors kept her under observation in a room for a month. They weren't able to explain how she went without food for so long. I've personally seen holy men, *sadhus,* who sleep standing on one leg, and weight lifters who pick up twelve-pound weights with their eyelids."

Then Bubbles added, "There's a place between Jaipur and Agra, Mahendipur, that frightens my wife. She refuses to go with me. They have people bound in chains who are possessed by evil spirits. They have incredible strength and are prevented from escaping by posts in the ground. I've seen 120 people chained on this avenue."

Bubbles hesitated. "There is a strangeness about the place. I've seen chained girls standing on their hands upside down and their skirts stay up, like invisible threads are pulling them towards the sky."

Not to be outdone, I said, "I've walked barefoot across burning coals."

"Really?" asked Ranveer.

"I've done it twice," I said. "The first time I took a cheap fire-walking seminar. I think it was the first time the person offered the course. He didn't inspire confidence. But I was determined. To graduate you walk across a twelve-foot pit of burning embers. When I stepped onto the coals I learned what it feels like to be a human hamburger. The pain was a hundred times worse than when I was ten and slipped on the jungle gym and did a crotch plant on the bottom bar."

"It sounds terrible," said Ranveer. "You did it twice?"

I nodded. "After my feet healed. I looked for another fire-walking instructor. People recommended a trainer named Anthony Robbins—a lot more expensive. Robbins says he doesn't know how it works, but if you follow his directions, most people make it across the BBQ without burning. I was scared. I didn't want to have medium rare feet a second time. I did everything he asked. Even then, I didn't walk first. I waited to see if other people made it across successfully. I'd talked with Robbins before the program and told him about my fear. He said he would tell me when he thought I was ready. When he said 'Go!', it was like walking across damp astro turf. Not even a sunburn on the bottom of my feet. The human body can do amazing things. I wouldn't recommend trying it unless you have an experienced trainer."

The next day we were out interviewing camels again. Eventually we narrowed down our camel choices to four: Grey Beard, Check Mark, Big Tongue, and Curly. Now was the time for a second opinion—a veterinarian's opinion.

Buying Used Camels

Several veterinarians helped us in our search for camels. Dr. Bhadani was the most memorable. The good doctor offered to inspect our camels before buying. This consisted of watching them walk and trot, viewing their teeth and eyes, running hands over their bodies, and listening to their hearts.

Assured by Dr. Bhadani that the camels we had chosen were in good health, we started bargaining with the owners. They were asking between 15,000 and 17,000 rupees per animal. This is about $300 U.S. We haggled to get the price lower, but no one would go below 15,000 rupees. This is about 5,000 rupees more than a local would pay. We could have bargained for another week and gotten them down lower, but we were eating up our riding time and decided it was a good price for them and we could afford it.

The traditional way of sealing a camel purchase is to give a small sum of money to the owner, and he hands you the reins to the camel. We repeated this process four times, going from home to home. By now it was 9:30 P.M. We wanted to sleep in the village that night, but the owners were anxious to get the rest of their money, which for safety we had left in the hotel back in Bikaner. They also made the sensible suggestion that it would be cooler to cross the desert at night, a distance of twenty miles following a sandy track.

Using the light from our headlamps, the villagers saddled the camels. Having done some camel riding in the States, I checked the girth and stomach hitches, trying to look like I knew what I was doing. Actually, I didn't have a clue. The saddles I'd used in the States were completely different. Little did Dan and I know that these saddles weren't riding saddles. They were designed to rest a yoke on to pull a wagon. We'd find out soon enough.

Three villagers accompanied us. They were in great spirits— smiling and joking—and probably commenting to each other what a great deal they had just made. They helped Dan and me get into the saddles. We wanted to do everything ourselves, but they didn't want to take a chance that one of us would get injured before they received final payment.

It's a rush when a camel rises up. The back legs come up first, which can catapult, or in this case, camelpult you from the saddle. I warned Dan to hold onto the saddle bar to avoid being thrown.

Then the front legs lurch up. The owners walked in front of the camels, holding the reins. As they led us through the village, Dan and I had as much control as two sacks of grain. But it was great. Eight feet off the ground, we could see over the walls of the villagers' homes. The families waved at us. We waved back enthusiastically. Eventually we came to a dirt track and entered the desert. It felt like the adventure had really started. We were crossing the desert at night. About then my rear end started to hurt.

The traditional way to agree on a camel price is to give the owner a small wad of cash as the owner hands you the reins. Dan, on the right, seals the deal on our first camel. One down, three to go.

Before leaving for India, many experienced people who had ridden a camel at a county fair for one minute and twenty-seven seconds, asked if I wasn't worried about a camel's uncomfortable ride. Having ridden for a number of days in Nevada, I replied, "When you get into the movement of the camel, it's easier than riding a horse." Of course I'd had a decent camel saddle then. The saddle I was sitting on now had all kinds of metal thingamajiggies that held together a rough wooden frame. One of the thingamajiggies was located where my tailbone met the wood. I folded a blanket up and put it between me and the annoying metal burr. Then I folded the blanket again. Not easy to do while riding on a swaying camel. Then I folded it again and added my folded jacket. Even then, I could feel it through the fabric, as in *The Princess and the Pea*, only this pea was a tiny dagger.

I did my best to concentrate on the landscape. In the darkness, the desert trees created fantastic silhouettes against the horizon—a stegosaurus, two chickens fighting, and a man astride a hippo. Dogs howled in the distance. Occasionally we passed a camel cart headed in the opposite direction. The drivers were sprawled on their loads, asleep while their homing-pigeon camels headed down the track to the village. I envied these sleeping drivers. My butt was beginning to feel like it had been whacked by a two-by-four. When the rubbing became intolerable, Dan and I walked while our guides rode. We arrived in town at the hotel at 4:30 A.M.

Dan arranged for tea for the camel sellers while I went up to our room. I searched through my luggage and pulled out one of our potato-chip-bag bank vaults. I counted out a stack of rupees to make our final payment for the camels. Bubbles came down to oversee the transfer. He wisely suggested a bill of sale to show we were the new camel owners and arranged for someone to watch the camels. Seven hours of night riding had left both Dan and me punchy. All we could think of was bed. Not our village escorts. They scooped the money up from the table, shook our hands, and with big smiles they headed towards town to party. Dan and I headed upstairs and collapsed on our beds.

"We did it," I said. "We are camel men."

"Brilliant, isn't it?" replied Dan sleepily.

"I wonder what the camels think about all this?"

"Probably nothing."

I wasn't so sure. As I drifted off to sleep I dreamed about the camels. This was their adventure too.

Camel Talk I

While walking with our animals, Dan and I often discussed what was going on in our humped herbivores' heads. The following camel conversations were inspired by actual events that occurred during the trip.

The four camels stood tied to blocks of concrete near a wall on the outskirts of Bikaner. Their eyes followed the forms of three familiar men, the food givers, who had taken care of them for years. The men walked away from the camels without looking back. The camels shifted from foot to foot. Long necks craned to take in the strangeness surrounding them. They would have preferred that their familiar food givers had remained near them. This place was unlike their desert home. The smell of hot asphalt, the thunk-thunk of motors, and the sight of buildings higher than any desert home they had ever seen, made them skittish.

The darkest of the camels, with curly hair, looked desperately after one of the departing humans. Then a woeful wail escaped her throat, "Something different, something bad. I so, so sad."

A camel, with a check-mark brand on one hip, turned towards the dark camel and mimicked disdainfully, "Something different, something bad. I so, so sad." Her nostrils flared in disgust. "That's the worst camel poetry I've ever heard."

The dark camel moaned, "Worry, worry, sorry, sorry."

Check Mark looked at the other two camels and sniffed, "They've put me next to the village idiot."

Standing next to the moaning dark camel was a fawn-colored beauty. In low tones she said, "She didn't mean it. She's just nervous like the rest of us."

Check Mark turned on Fawn. "I mean just what I say. I don't need an interpreter unless I'm talking to an ignorant water buffalo. What herd did they find you in?"

Shyly, Fawn replied, "I was village born."

"Oh, a peasant camel," said Check Mark. "I should have known. I've never seen such spindly legs. If you didn't have a hump, I'd think you were a dumb desert gazelle. Just so you understand. I'm a high-caste camel and will not tolerate a lower-caste camel contradicting me. I will bite your neck if you do it again."

Fawn lowered her head.

Taking the lowered head as a sign of submission, Check Mark added, "At least you know how to behave around your superiors." She turned towards the remaining camel, who sported a grey beard under her chin.

Grey Beard did not lower her head. She had hauled carts through the desert weighing over 1,000 pounds. She was twice as old as the other camels and desert smart. She stood her ground as Check Mark pivoted towards her.

"And what do you have to say about our situation?" asked Check Mark.

Grey Beard calmly returned Check Mark's challenging gaze and said, "It is going to change."

"What does that mean?" asked Check Mark.

"We aren't returning home," said Grey Beard.

"Nonsense," huffed Check Mark. "My food giver will be coming back to get me shortly. I will be returning home."

Grey Beard made no comment.

Grey Beard was right. The old food givers didn't return that day or any day after that.

Members of the International Desert Animal Welfare Society of India

We'd only managed a few hours of sleep after riding across the desert when there was a knock at our door.

"Go away," groaned Dan.

"You have a visitor," came a voice from the other side of the door.

"Won't it wait?" asked Dan.

"Dr. Bhadani is waiting in the foyer. What do you want me to tell him?"

"Blast it," Dan paused. "Tell him we will be down in a minute."

"He probably wants to be paid," I said.

We dragged ourselves out of bed and went down to meet Dr. Bhadani. He was all smiles and handshakes. We ordered tea and slumped down on a couch in the hotel lobby. Bubbles's dog came over looking for attention. I avoided touching most dogs in India as they often cool off by lying in sewage filled gutters. Not Bubbles's pooch, a well-scrubbed hotel dog. As I scratched his head, Dr. Bhadani told us how much we owed him. I stopped scratching the dog. The price he quoted would gag a Maharaja. We were being ripped off. It was partly our fault. We hadn't settled on a price prior to his services. At this point, Dan and I made excuses to leave the foyer. We needed time to figure out how to handle the rip off. While we were gone, we think Bubbles, or someone from the hotel staff, stepped in and had a word with the doctor.

When we came back in, Dr. Bhadani eyed Bubbles at the lobby desk and turned to us, "I would like to waive my fees. You are on a humanitarian mission to help people. I myself have a charity. I think we can help each other. I will donate my veterinary services." He paused, "In return, I would like to ask your assistance with my foundation, the *International Desert Animal Welfare Society of India*. The fee to join is 500 rupees ($10 U.S.). Much less than the veterinarian bill."

"So let me get this straight," I said. "We pay 500 rupees to join your foundation and you drop the veterinarian costs?"

"Yes," said Dr. Bhadani, "And, if you would make out a receipt for the veterinarian costs to show that I have donated my services. This is for tax purposes."

Dan and I looked at each other sideways. Dan nodded. Seemed like a good deal.

"Plus assistance?" said Dr. Bhadani hopefully.

"Assistance?" I asked warily.

"You will promote my foundation with publicity," said Dr. Bhadani.

"And how will we do that?" I asked.

"I will make a banner that your camels will carry," explained Dr. Bhadani. "It will list the tenets of the *International Desert Animal Welfare Society of India.*"

"And what are the tenets?" I asked.

"Tenet one encourages the humane treatment of camels," said Dr. Bhadani.

Dan and I nodded. We could go along with that.

"Tenet two asks that you stroke domestic animals to show affection. It is good for both the animal and the owner."

"OK."

"Tenet three says you will advocate the drinking of cow and camel urine every day. I myself drink at least a cupful daily. It is a healthy practice that fortifies the body and builds the immune system. As a regular practice, it can extend the human life span to 200 years. I hope to live to be 200."

Dr. Bhadani went through a few more tenets, but I was hung up on the third one. When he finished, I said, "Would you excuse us for a minute. I need to talk to Dan."

Dr. Bhadani smiled and leaned back on the couch.

In private, Dan said, "I'm willing to go along with the banner if it means we can skip paying the vet costs. Only one thing—you get to drink the pee."

"Thanks Dan," I said. "But I want you to live to be 200 years old along with me."

Dan chuckled.

"Look," I continued, "the tenet advocates the drinking of urine. I don't think the word 'advocate' means you actually have to do the drinking."

"Good point," said Dan. "I have a suggestion."

"What's that?" I asked.

"We don't accept a dinner invitation from Dr. Bhadani," said Dan. "Never know what he might serve for drinks."

Dan and I signed on the dotted line and became members of the *International Desert Animal Welfare Society of India*. We suspect it is an elite group with few members.

The Camel Hospital

As members of Dr. Bhadani's foundation, we were offered further services, which included a series of shots to protect our camels from various ailments and parasites. We were given an address and an appointment. It wasn't far from the hotel where we were staying.

A visit to the veterinary hospital where he worked was a one-time event. As we led our camels into the courtyard, I had immediate misgivings. I tend to avoid going to hospitals. I feel that you only visit a hospital if you have no other choice to save life or limb. After all, hospitals are where sick people go. What better place to pick up a disease? This vet hospital was out of the dark ages with a few modern items thrown in, such as used syringes and broken medication bottles littering the grounds. Sick animals with oozing noses occupied the waiting area. Six men were struggling with a water buffalo that didn't seem to be able to stand up. The fleas were so bad our camels started kicking and leaping about. I looked at Dan and vehemently said, "We're out of here."

When Dr. Bhadani stopped by later to inquire why we had left so quickly, I didn't mince words about standards of care. After all I was now a card-carrying member of the *International Desert Animal Welfare Society of India,* and I didn't feel the hospital had the welfare of our animals in mind. To his credit he offered to make a house call and give the shots our camels needed from the supplies we had. He also inquired if we had started drinking animal urine. I told him we were waiting for the right moment to get started. He told us he was having the banner made.

Night Watchman

Because our camels were tethered across the street from the hotel and out in the open, Bubbles suggested we hire a night watchman. A watchman could help feed the camels and watch over them at night so we didn't have a camel kidnapping. Bubbles had a family friend in mind. He'd known the man since he was a child. This watchman could also help us train the camels.

That afternoon we met Katea-ram-ji. Katea-ram came up to my chest. It looked like he was having a crazy hair day. His shoulder-length, wild raven black hair and matching beard stuck out in all directions. His moustache curled over his ears, barely concealing his smile. Since Katea-ram didn't speak English, Bubbles acted as interpreter to help us set the deal.

"Katea-ram says he is on a two-month-long fast," interpreted Bubbles. "He would be happy to help take care of your camels, but you will have to watch them when he goes to prayers. He's a camel man so he will also help you train the camels. I have suggested a per day price of 150 rupees [about $3 U.S.]."

At that point Katea-ram interrupted.

"He also says that part of the deal will include lassis, tea, and cigarettes," said Bubbles.

"What does that mean?" asked Dan.

"Well, Katea-ram believes that he will die without his smokes, so you will need to stock up on cigarettes. You will also provide him with tea and lassis."

"What is a lassi?" I asked.

"It is a milk, yogurt, and banana drink."

"I thought he was on a fast?"

"Oh, it is a fast where he eats no solid food."

I looked at Dan. "Remember that lady Ranveer told us about? The one who didn't eat anything but a leaf a day? I wonder if her fast included tea and milkshakes?"

We were to discover that a "fasting" Katea-ram could put away eight cups of tea liberally laced with milk and sugar and up to six banana lassis a day. And while he might believe that he would die without his smokes, his hacking spitting-up-sputum cough suggested that cigarettes were polluting his lungs the same way they do in the U.S.

One of Katea-ram's first lessons for us was that Katea-ram is right. Dan and I are wrong. This wasn't done meanly. More like a kindly old uncle trying to teach his dim-witted nephews. In the beginning, we were unable to satisfy him on the simplest tasks. He showed us how to tie a camel to a tree. There are two ways—the Katea-ram way and the wrong way. We were constantly scolded for tying this knot the wrong way. Dan swears that Katea-ram changed the knot each time he corrected us to keep us off balance. Considering that Dan is a certified master climbing instructor and knows how to tie knots more complex than a Rubik's cube, I thought he had a point. But we nodded humbly and dumbly as we tried to satisfy our teacher.

Katea-ram, our night watchman and soon to be good friend.

While Katea-ram could make us crazy, we were also fond of him. The first time we rode into town on a camel cart to get food for our little herd, the locals waved at us like we were on a float in the Rose Parade. They were probably surprised to see foreigners on anything that wasn't motorized. The three of us waved back wildly. Judging from the smile on Katea-ram's face, he was having as much fun as we were. It also cracked me up when Katea-ram would carry on full conversations with us in rapid Hindi. We didn't have a clue as to what he was saying. Dan would come right back at him with full conversations in the Queen's English, which I'm sure were equally unintelligible to Katea-ram. But it never stopped the two of them from "babble talk." Katea-ram seemed to simply enjoy the interaction. Dan was simply being wicked.

Camel School

Now that we had camels, we had to figure out what to do with them. First, we gave them names. As I've already mentioned, villagers don't name their animals. This meant any names we gave the camels wouldn't confuse them. This would be the first time they had names. Our oldest camel, who was eight to ten years old, had a small tuft of white hairs sprouting from her chin. At first we named her Grey Beard—we were being really creative—but Dan shortened it to GB, which he said stood for Great Britain. Raika, the camel with a check mark brand, got her name from the desert tribe where we first tried to buy camels. Sam, the fawn colored beauty, was a name provided by one of our sponsors. And then there was Humper Jack, the darkest camel, again named by a sponsor. We called her Humper for short. As the weeks passed, we learned that each camel had a personality. Their traits went from calm grandma to tantruming teenager.

During our camel search, Dan and I discovered that camels trained to be ridden on city streets are a rare commodity. Most Indian camels pull carts, plough fields, or give milk. Those that are used for tourist safaris are ridden in a desert environment where there aren't any vehicles. Bubbles tried to convince us to buy a cart and a camel trained to pull a cart.

Camel carts in India carry up to 2,000 pounds. This cart is returning to a village with a supply of firewood collected in the desert.

"If you have a cart you can load all your supplies on the cart and carry camel feed for a number of days so you won't have to search for food," Bubbles reasonably explained. "It will also be easier to find a camel trained to pull a cart than one trained for riding."

"It doesn't sound very exciting," I said. "Bumping along in a cart all day long is not what I imagined."

While I wasn't keen on the idea of a cart, Dan liked it. "Remember those guys we saw who were sleeping on their carts while the camels took them home?" said Dan. "One of us could kick back in the cart and the other one could ride a camel."

I wasn't swayed. "What happens if we want to go off-track? A cart would force us to find a well-traveled route. Remember when you were worried it wouldn't be an adventure because I'd done too much planning? If we had a cart we would be stuck on tracks and roads. Where's the adventure in that? Remember how we were going to gallop across India?"

I also argued that carts were expensive. Then there was the problem of a break down and finding spare parts in the middle of the desert. I don't think I ever fully convinced Dan, but eventually he agreed, no cart, just camels.

Now we were faced with training our four camels so that we could ride them near traffic they would meet on the road and in cities.

We had two training choices. The *whacker* or the *clicker* technique. First the whacker method. Animals don't have rights in India as they do in the U.S. There is no Animal Planet Police Force that punishes cruel owners. In India we saw midget donkeys pulling over-sized carts. To get the donkeys to keep a quick pace, owners scrape the flesh off near the base of the donkey's tail. To get an animal to move, the driver takes a sharp stick and snaps the open wound. Ouch! We also saw a cart handler who carried a brick. When his horse was stubborn, the driver whacked the rump of the horse with the brick. Two of our camels, Humper and Sam, had obviously been trained with harsh techniques. Whenever Humper saw a raised hand she started moaning. Sam, seeing a hand or walking stick near her head, would shy away as if ready for a blow. Sam and Humper had obviously been whacker trained.

Our second choice was clicker training. It is a humane way to get animals to do what you want. Karen Pryor introduced me to the technique. She first used the technique to train dolphins and killer whales for sea life park shows. Since then she has advised people on how to use it on horses, dogs, cats, parrots, giraffes, rhinos, even a hermit crab. Clicker training requires a clicker, target stick, and lots of treats. For example if you want a camel to come to you and put its nose into your hand, you hold up the target stick, a short stick with a tennis ball on the end. When, out of curiosity, the camel moves in the direction of the stick, you click and give the animal a treat. The animal soon learns to pay attention to the stick and click. After each success, the target stick is moved closer to your hand. Eventually a verbal or hand signal takes the place of the target stick, and the animal puts its nose in your hand for a click and treat. I think of myself as a vending machine and the animal is trying to figure out what behavior will get the vending machine to drop its treat. I tried out clicker training on the camel herd I worked with in Nevada. The results were good.

Prior to coming to India, I practiced clicker training techniques on camels in Nevada. The camel has been taught to move her head towards the ball on the end of the target stick to obtain a treat.

To get more clicker-training practice, I bought three ducks. Ducks are not particularly smart. Yet, over the summer I clicker trained the ducks so they would enter their pen on command. One duck learned to pick up a little barbell and put it in my hand. I taught my smartest duck to dance. He'd spin in a circle depending on which way I circled my hand. I looked forward to trying the technique on Indian camels.

Try out clicker training for yourself

To practice clicker training, all you need is a clicker, a bag of M&Ms, and a willing person. One of you will be the trainer, with the clicker and the treats. The other person is the camel. Decide on a simple "trick" to teach your partner. But don't tell him what it is. Maybe you want him to put his hand on his head, or stand on one foot. Then start. When the person makes any move even close to what you want you immediately click and give him an M&M. After reinforcing this behavior a few times, withhold the click and treat. Your "camel" may seem confused. He will try what paid off before, but no treat. When in his trials he does something closer to what you want, start the click and treat sequence again. Eventually he is clicked all the way to your goal.

When Katea-ram observed my first clicker training session with the camels, he quickly made up his mind about the technique.

Hardly able to contain himself, Katea-ram snorted, "It is the silliest thing I have seen. If you want a disobedient camel to obey you, simply double pierce the camel's nose and put a needle into the second hole. When you pull hard on the reins, it will be so painful, the animal will do whatever you want."

I'd seen this method used on some of the cart camels in Bikaner. The drivers weren't taking any chances on losing control of their animals in the city. I flinched, along with the camels, whenever I saw these drivers pull on their reins.

"No way," I said. "I want our camels to like us."

"A camel does not obey you because he likes you," lectured Katea-ram. "But, they are your camels."

I'm sure that Katea-ram thought I was a block-headed doofus for ignoring his advice. He was particularly gratified during one of my clicker training sessions with Raika. Raika had quickly learned how to earn treats by moving towards the target stick. I smirked at Katea-ram who stood nearby watching the training. Then, without warning, Raika grabbed the protective ball on the end of the target stick and sucked it into her mouth. Fearing she'd swallow it and choke to death, I thrust my hand into her mouth. A tug of war ensued. Displeased with the hand in her mouth, Raika made a decision. Suddenly, she spewed the remains of a partly digested meal from her mouth. Slimy green cud splattered on to my head and chest. Standing there—with the retrieved ball in my hand—I wiped camel barf from my face as Katea-ram laughed so hard, I thought he'd have a stroke.

In general, Dan and I were kind to our camels. But like parents who swear they will never spank their child—there were times when we lost control. If I had been a more experienced clicker trainer I might have overcome my frustration. But even simple clicker skills were challenging. In the States I used pieces of apples or carrots for treats. American camels love apples and carrots. Indian camels like apples and carrots as much as kids like bitter cough syrup. It was not until I admitted to Katea-ram that I was the village idiot that he showed me the Keker Pali tree. The long bean pods of the tree have a lemony taste that Indian camels relish. Dan and I became skilled at climbing into the trees to collect the pods. But everything takes time and we didn't have a lot of time before we needed to leave.

It wasn't only the camels that were going to school. Dan and I were being educated by Katea-ram. Our first lesson included Indian camel commands. To get a camel to kneel down so you can mount, you make a breathy "Jai" sound. Katea-ram would make the sound and a camel would drop like it had been hit with a sledge-hammer. Dan and I made the identical sound and the camel stared at us unmoving. "Go" is a popping sound with the tongue on the palate—a moderately useful command. To tell a camel to go faster, you tap your heels against the camel's sides. "Back" is *pach*. "Stop" is a kissing sound—the most worthless command. There were many times when we were galloping madly through town desperately sucking our lips into our windpipes trying to make the kissing sound heard.

We were also being taught how to saddle, feed, clean, and ride. Riding was the most exciting. Part of the excitement came from having a riding instructor who spoke no English. On Dan's first city ride, Katea-ram handed him the reins. They were crossed under the camel's chin. Dan sensibly uncrossed them. Katea-ram said something. Dan didn't understand. Katea-ram shrugged. Apparently, Katea-ram had said the reins were to remain crossed, that's why he handed them to Dan that way. When Dan and mount reached the street, a bus came by, blaring its horn. GB took one look at the approaching bus and bolted into traffic, going at a full gallop, head-on toward swerving cars, trucks, motorcycles, and autorickshaws, with Katea-ram chasing behind in flip-flops. Dan pulled back on the reins, which only pulled the camel's head high into the air (crossed reins would have put more pressure on the camel's nose pegs and may have stopped the animal). Katea-ram yelled in Hindi for Dan to stop. Dan, clutching the saddle to avoid being thrown to the street in front of the swerving traffic, yelled back words that he only uses when stressed.

Dan went for a wild ride when he lost control of his camel in traffic.

Nothing brings greater pleasure to an Indian pedestrian than the sight of a foreigner clinging to an out-of-control camel galloping down a city street. They laughed so hard they had to support one another. When Dan's camel finally stopped, much to Dan's relief, a crowd of 150 people surrounded him, laughing and miming his wild ride. Dan was the talk of the town.

Camel Talk II

The food giver's face was flushed. He had the fear smell. He tied GB up next to the other camels and yanked off her saddle. GB had signs of spittle foam on her mouth like she had been ridden hard.

"What happened to you?" asked Raika.

"The food giver almost got us killed," breathed GB. "He took us close to the giant dung beetles' paths. I have seen the smaller dung beetles many times—some two-legs ride in their bellies. But I've never seen any this big. Some were the size of sand dunes. They moved with no legs I could see, and faster than a gazelle. Their foul odor signals danger to any sane creature. One came right at me and made a sound like a monstrous goose. My food giver pulled on my pegs, but his pull didn't make sense. I had no choice. I followed the first camel god commandment—run from danger as fast and far as you can."

"Smart, smart, smart," said Humper.

"You did the right thing," said Raika. "These food givers have less brains than a thorn tree. The other day I almost taught the thin food giver a lesson. He was acting very odd. He held a stick in front of my nose. On the end there was something green. It looked like a small melon. I pulled it off the stick and tried to swallow it." Raika paused. The other camels nodded at her sensible behavior. Then she continued, "The food giver dropped the stick and stuck his hand inside my mouth. Before I could do anything, I felt his hand slide across my tongue. He grabbed the melon and pulled it out of my mouth. I had half a mind to chomp down on his arm."

"Why didn't you?" asked GB.

"The melon tasted strange," replied Raika. "It had a taste I may not have wanted in my stomach so I let him take it."

"It sounds like a strange if not stupid thing to do," said GB.

"Oh, my food giver is not completely stupid," said Raika. "I taught him a trick. Whenever I touch the melon that is not a melon on the end of the stick, he gives me lemony pods. They are delicious. He learned this trick quickly. But if he takes me near the giant beetles, I may have to push him into the beetles' path. If one food giver gets flattened, the other may stay away from the beetles."

"Then you would have no food giver," said Sam timidly. She knew it was a mistake as soon as she voiced her comment.

"Well that shouldn't concern you," said Raika. "I notice the food givers are uninterested in you two. Only GB and I receive their attention while you two remain tied to trees. The only reason I can see for them wasting feed on you is that they are fattening you up before they eat you."

At that Humper groaned loudly.

"Food givers don't eat camels," blurted out Sam.

"Yes they do," said Raika meanly. "I still remember the death smell. They took one of our kind and burned him over a fire. Then they pulled him apart and stuffed their little mouths with his flesh."

"They don't do this," said Sam turning to GB.

GB only turned away.

Katea-ram's Joke

During our lessons Katea-ram loved joking. It was simple humor. He'd ask me to hold out my hand and then put a camel turd on my open palm. Seeing the look of disgust on my face, he'd start chortling, grab my hand in his own, and jabber away at me in Hindi. The biggest joke he played on us was getting hired to teach us how to ride camels. I had just galloped down a city street on Raika, completely out of control with Katea-ram yelling instructions at me in Hindi. Finally, I bailed out, leaping from the saddle at a full run and barely managing to keep my feet under me. I was not in a good mood. I was hot, a little scared, and frustrated by Katea-ram's confusing commands.

"First you tell me to do one thing," I fumed, "Then you tell me to do something completely different." I threw him the reins and said, "You ride."

Katea-ram looked at Raika doubtfully. He mounted her with as much care as someone working on a bomb squad. Cautiously he goaded her in the ribs to move forward. But Raika was in one of her moods. Rather than Katea-ram taking Raika for a ride, Raika took Katea-ram for a ride. Commanded to go forward, she instead backed up madly trying to scrape Katea-ram off on a nearby wall. Katea-ram held on with a white-knuckled death-grip. As she cranked up to full bronco mode, she became a swirling tornado, trying to dislodge the pest on her back. Then suddenly, without warning, she stopped. Her head snaked around, as only a camel can do, and she gave Katea-ram the Clint Eastwood stare—translation: "Do you feel lucky, punk? Well, do you? Make my day." Katea-ram hastily slid off and refused to ever ride one of our camels again. His ego bruised, he said, "It's too dangerous for an old man." It turned out that, while Katea-ram knew cart camels, he was a camel-riding beginner. True to his word, he never got on one of the camels again.

Regardless of the problems we had, Katea-ram was worth every penny we paid him. He taught us how to hobble, feed, kneel, mount, saddle, pack, and nose-peg a camel. Nose-pegging was scary. Nose pegs are based on The Three Stooges principle. If you are a Stooge fan, you know that the fastest way to control Moe, Larry, or Curly was to grab one of them by the nose. This is because human noses have low pain tolerance. Camel nose pegs are supposed to work in a similar stooge-like fashion. Pull on the peg and you get the camel's attention. Sam managed to break both of her nose pegs in our first day of ownership. Dan and I were indirectly to blame for the accident. We had decided to take GB and Raika for a walk around town. Humper and Sam were left tied up in front of the hotel. What we didn't anticipate was that camels are incredibly social, and our team of four had already bonded. Sam was so distressed when she saw the other two camels leave that she pulled on her reins until she broke both of her pegs, in order to follow us. When she caught up with us and we saw the damaged nose pegs, Dan and I looked at each other like two kids who'd broken the neighbor's window. Dan ran to find Katea-ram while I put a temporary halter around Sam's neck.

Katea-ram looked at the two broken nose pegs and went off to collect a group of local men. The men tied Sam's legs together. Hobbled, she wouldn't be able to kick. Camels are black belt kick-ers. They can kick in all directions—front, side, or back. Five men held Sam's head. A new nose peg, which had a shape similar to the bishop in a chess set, was coated in mustard oil to make it slip in easier. Then Wrestlemania began. Imagine someone trying to shove a wedge of wood halfway up your nostril, and then turn it ninety degrees, so it can be forced through a slit in your snout. This is serious body piercing. Sam roared, bared her teeth, and shook off the five men. It took several attempts before the operation was successful. Dan and I had been left to observe. I was completely cowed (cameled?). We considered having all the nose pegs replaced, similar to replacing all the tires on a car, in the hopes we wouldn't have to change a peg during the expedition. Operating on a 1,400 pound patient without anesthesia is scary. Katea-ram talked us out of the replacement. Replaced pegs take time to heal. I prayed we wouldn't have to do it on the trip. It was a prayer that would be ignored later on.

Shopping Spree

In between our work with the camels, Dan and I were mall rats. There were lots of things to buy for the expedition. At first we were overwhelmed by what seemed a hodgepodge system of shops. After careful study, we found that shops are arranged like major car dealerships in the U.S. There is a concentration of leather workers in one area; blacksmiths occupy another street, often near coal sellers; fresh produce vendors cluster in another location; camel supplies are located on another street. To help us find these areas, we hired an autorickshaw driver and Vijay, an interpreter, to help with the negotiations. We had to explain to the blacksmith how to make the stirrups we needed. I often used my drawing skills to make a picture of what we wanted built. A tailor was employed to make panniers, a sort of camel backpack. To explain our pannier design, I built a scale model of a camel out of plastic soda bottles and the packs out of paper and glue. We also designed a halter, a series of straps that could be slipped over a camel's head to lead it, and gave the plans to a leather worker. Equipment was being made for us all over town.

An ironworker making a set of stirrups for our riding saddles. Indian saddles usually don't have stirrups, but we felt that having a place to put our feet, like on a horse saddle, would make it harder for a camel to throw us. Many of the craftsmen we hired, like the one pictured here, used simple tools to manufacture a variety of goods. Often there were hazards. This workman isn't wearing safety goggles or gloves, but he did protect his bare feet from hot embers with a piece of an old sack.

Wealthy foreigners

A number of shopkeepers doubled or tripled the prices of items when they saw Dan or me enter their stores. In the shopkeepers' minds, foreigners are wealthy and wouldn't mind the extra cost. To keep from being overcharged, Dan and I learned to look for prices marked on items (although it didn't do us much good when it was written in Hindi as neither of us reads Hindi), asked locals what the price should be, or offered half the price when something seemed out of line. Haggling over prices is common when shopping, although it doubles the time it takes to make a purchase.

And we did feel wealthy in India. If I were back in America and had gone to McDonald's for a meal, then taken in a movie with popcorn, soda, and candy, I'd have spent as much or more than the average Indian makes in a month. In Rajasthan, a state in India, farmers earn 500 rupees ($10 U.S.) a month. A servant in a home works seven days a week without a break and gets 1,000 rupees ($20 U.S.) a month. A hotel worker earns about 4,500 rupees ($90 U.S.) a month. Considering the low wages, fortunately the cost of items in India is also much less than the US:

Item	Cost in India	Cost in the U.S.
Bar of soap	$0.08	$2.00
Bottle of 7-UP	$0.14	$1.00
Loaf of bread	$0.10	$2.50
Movie ticket	$0.40	$10.00
2.2 lbs. bananas	$0.20	$1.80
Watermelon	$0.10	$3.00
2 qts. of milk	$0.24	$4.00
Live chicken	$2.00	$10.00
A sheep	$40.00	$400.00
Camel	$300.00	$10,000.00

We had the most fun shopping at the camel accessory store. Here we picked through saddles, grain bags, padding, blankets, hobbles, nose pegs, halters, girth straps, and reins. My experience with horses and limited experience with American camel supplies was all we had to go on. Most of our purchases relied on common sense. Looking at palans (saddles), we noted that they were identical in shape to ceremonial saddles in the Jungaragh Fort Museum in Bikaner. In other words, nothing had changed over the centuries. The best palans weren't on view. A dark hole in the floor led to a broom-closet-sized cellar jammed with saddles. A saddle with all the padding cost about 1,000 rupees, just $20. These saddles weren't designed for riding long distances. Too many sharp angles and metal studs. Comfortable riding saddles weren't available in Bikaner. Ranveer came to our rescue.

A stack of wooden camel saddles. The addition of blankets, padding, and straps complete the saddle.

"You will need proper saddles," said Ranveer. "With these camel cart saddles you will not ride far. At my hotel we have saddles. I bought them at the Pushkar Fair, where they have the best riding equipment. We use them for guests who wish to play polo on camels instead of horses. They will be much better suited to your adventure. I will have two dropped off at the hotel."

Again, we were humbled by the generosity of those we met in India. Everyone wanted to make our trip a success.

Our departure was fast approaching.

"Dan," I said, "I don't know about you but I'm not feeling all that prepared. I think we are going to need some help on the trail, at least for the first week or two."

"I agree," replied Dan. "Maybe we can get Katea-ram to come with us. He could help us find food for the camels in the villages along the way. And I still have a heck of a time getting GB to kneel."

At first Katea-ram shook his head. No. He had never been more than a short distance from Bikaner. It would be a hard trip and he was still "fasting." Bubbles intervened on our behalf and had a talk with Katea-ram. Finally Katea-ram agreed, but added "I will not ride the camels."

Our little expedition gained one more person after an incident with Katea-ram. After the nose-pegging operation, Katea-ram took us to a tiny shop, sort of an animal drug store. Here he picked through a tray of nose pegs. In the meantime, the shopkeeper brought out a box. He showed it to Katea-ram who passed it to us. The box held chunks of a resinous material. Dan and I tried to get Katea-ram to explain what the material was for with no success. We assumed it was some kind of camel medicine. The shop owner dropped three pieces into Dan's hands and asked for 150 rupees ($3 U.S.). I said, "It would be a good idea to get more for any problems we might have on the trail." Dan went into bargaining mode. He got a whole bag of the stuff for 50 rupees ($1 U.S.). We were feeling pretty clever about our dealings with the shop owner. Arriving back at the hotel, an interpreter explained that the substance was incense, and had no use for what we were doing. Katea-ram had no idea why we bought it. At this point, Dan and I decided we needed an interpreter, at least for the first part of the trip, to avoid similar misunderstandings.

Bubbles had a hard time persuading anyone from the hotel staff to accompany us. They thought it would be hard and dangerous. We tried to get Vijay to come as interpreter. He had been a great help when we bargained in town, but his family was concerned and said, "No." Finally, Bubbles introduced us to Iqrar, a part time safari guide and interpreter. He agreed to sign on for a couple of weeks. He would also help us practice our Hindi so that when we were on our own we could speak to the locals.

Learning languages is an important adventurer skill. Before the trip, I used a special memory technique to learn 186 Hindi words in a few days. These were words that would allow Dan and me to communicate basic needs: water, camel, food, left, right, HELP! The special memory technique I used made it possible to learn the Hindi words in a third the time it would normally take.

The Say-See-Stick Method for Learning a Foreign Language

You can learn a foreign language by repeating words over and over again, known as rote learning—the slowest way to learn a language—or you can use mnemonics. Mnemonics (pronounced knee-MON-iks) are techniques that improve memory. Here's how say-see-stick mnemonics are used for memorizing the Hindi word for water, pronounced *panee*. First you *say* the word aloud and listen for similarities to an English word. In this case pan is similar to the English word pan. Next you see in your mind's eye a pan. The *stick* comes when you glue the meaning of the word to the image you have in your mind. In this case, put water in the pan. Now when you need the word for water you think, where is the water? It's in a pan. The Hindi word begins with *pan* and you have the beginning of the word. You could also have the pan resting on a knee (pan knee) to get the full sound of the word, but I find if I have a place to start, the foreign word often comes back to me. If you'd like to see more Hindi words turned into memorable images with the say-see-stick method, turn to Appendix A.

Charming Cobras

While preparing for the expedition, I made a list of 100 goals to accomplish during the trip (see Appendix B for the full list). Goals on my list included: #1 buy four camels, #3 wear a turban, #11 ride through Sariska Tiger Reserve, #18 get a camel blessed, #28 meet an untouchable, and #41 charm a cobra. Bubbles liked #41. Taking a break from camel training, Bubbles arranged for Dan and me to train cobras.

Our snake teacher arrived dressed in a white turban, bright orange jacket, and white *dhouti* (skirt-like pants). His clothing indicated that he followed the Nath religion. The cobra is part of that religion. Every two to three months this master of snakes collects a black cobra from the wild. These serpents can be as thick as a man's arm and up to seven feet long. Using a secret religious prayer, or mantra, he calms and trains the snake. This takes two to three days. He then cares for the snake, and the snake, through performances and donations provided by the audience, cares for the snake charmer. At the end of a period determined by astrological signs, the cobra is returned to the wild. Our tutor carried several baskets under his arms. He set one on the ground in front of me. As he removed the lid, I instinctively stepped back.

There was no mistaking the deadly gun metal black coil inside the basket. The snake charmer sat nonchalantly next to the basket and tapped the snake on the head with his finger. The performance is the one seen a thousand times a day across India. The snake rose into the air swaying to the melody of the snake charmer's flute.

Dan and I heard that many snake charmers are simply performers. It is not a religion. The snakes are not sacred, but just a tool, like the flute, used to lure money from tourists' pockets. To protect themselves, these performers rip the fangs out of their cobras. These mutilated cobras will die within a month or two. This wasn't the case for the cobras we were training with. According to the charmer, his religion forbids milking the venom from the snake or removing the fangs. Using a matchstick, snake man gently levered the venom fangs forward so we could clearly see them. "Yes," I said. "Those look like fangs to me." He assured us this was a fully loaded cobra to be treated with respect. Then it was my turn.

The flute used by snake charmers looks a bit like a cobra. Supposedly this resemblance helps to keep the real snake's attention.

I approached the snake like a sprinter on the blocks, ready to run in the opposite direction. It took some time before I was comfortable enough to sit cross-legged in front of the basket containing the snake. I puffed on the traditional flute. The snake rose into the air as if pulled by an invisible thread. The cobra was less than a foot away. It stared at me. I stared back as it flattened the upper part of its body in agitation. The snake doesn't actually boogie to the music, but rather sways to the hypnotic motion of the flute. As long as the flute keeps weaving, the snake won't strike. I'm not sure if it was the hyperventilated puffing into the flute or the weaving pattern that caused me to feel light-headed. I thought, *Great. What would happen if I passed out and fell head first into the snake basket?* When I was a kid I remembered watching a documentary film in which an Asian woman kissed a swaying king cobra on the head. The ritual required that she do it seven times. The idea of going head to head, tête-a-tête, with a poisonous snake freaked me out. Little did I know I would soon face that fear.

I asked to see how the snake was fed while under the snake charmer's care. He reached for a box. I expected a lunchbox filled with mousie meals. Instead, he produced a hollow bone. This was inserted into the snake's mouth. He then poured milk down this makeshift funnel. As the snake's body filled with milk, the man stroked the cobra to move the milk into its stomach. He has been doing this for over twenty years. His father did the same before him.

Dan commented, "I bet he doesn't worry about burglars. You know how we thought about getting a dog for protection? Maybe we should carry a couple of cobras in our bags. Wouldn't that be a surprise to a thief rummaging through our luggage?"

I then went from working with a snake in a basket to holding the snake in my hands. I did this cautiously. At one point, while I held the snake at the midpoint of its body, it turned back menacingly towards my hand. I dropped it with a resounding thwap on the paving stones. Snake man squinted at me and shook his head. This was not good snake-handling etiquette. I paid for my fear by learning how to apologize to a cobra. Holding the coiled snake in my hands, I touched it to my forehead. Eventually, I had it wrapped around my neck. As a necklace it makes a strong fashion statement. Bubbles displayed his lack of fear by pulling open his collar and letting the snake slither down inside his shirt.

To apologize to a cobra, I was taught to hold the snake and touch its head to my forehead.

Later we were shown a freshly caught cobra. This one uncoiled menacingly from the basket with no prodding. Even a beginning charmer like me noted the aggressive movements. Our snake-charming teacher was not as relaxed with this serpent. A little voice in my head said *you don't want that snake wrapped around your neck.*

Desert Internet

During the training, buying, and preparation for departure, I also spent time on the hotel's rooftop. This was the best place to sweat like a pig. It was also the best place for a bright sun to recharge our solar panel batteries. The batteries in turn powered our computer and satellite phone. This equipment supported goal #95 on my goal list: Maintain an Internet site so that school children around the world can follow our expedition. The technical equipment was the most frustrating part of the trip. Early on I discovered that the solar panels could not be mounted on moving camels. Loaded camels like to roll in the sand, which would destroy the panels. This meant we could only recharge our batteries in camp during rest days. Another headache was that the system had more bugs than a scorpion's nest. Battling Internet problems in the middle of the desert made me crazy. Dan discretely disappeared whenever he saw me unloading the Internet equipment.

On one of those days when I was wrestling with the computer, Dan slipped quietly out the door with Bubbles. They said they were going for a drive. Maybe Dan could get some photos of desert wildlife. What they were really doing was going hunting. Hunting is frowned on in this part of India, so local hunters have a secret code. When they say, "Do you want to go shoot some animal photos?" leave out the word photo and you understand what they are up to. Racing across the desert in a jeep, shooting at anything that moved, someone managed to shoot off the car's side view mirror. That night for dinner we were served rabbit, which Dan proudly told me he had "shot" with his camera.

Bubbles was full of surprises. Sometimes when we hired autorickshaw drivers to take us around Bikaner, we would casually

mention we were staying with Bubbles Singh and how he was helping us out.

"Bubbles Singh," responded the autorickshaw driver. "He is a
very good man."

Shop owners made the same comment. Why did so many
people know and like Bubbles? I've been told that someone who
respects you says good things about you behind your back. It
sounded like Bubbles had many people who respected him. Our
limited Hindi made it difficult to discover what was behind this
respect. Then one night we got the rest of the story.

Before our departure, Bubbles invited us to dinner at the hotel's
roof-top restaurant. We sat at a table under the open sky. Local
musicians played traditional Indian music. Looking out over the
city lights we started talking.

"Bubbles," I asked. "Bikaner seems awfully close to the Pakistan
border. Maybe sixty miles away. I know that India and Pakistan
have not been on friendly terms in the past. Has there ever been a
problem here in Bikaner?"

"Yes," said Bubbles. "The politicians got us very close to war.
Some years ago it became quite heated. Just outside of Bikaner, the
military set up a staging depot. Trucks loaded with ammunition,
rockets, and bombs came in one after another. There were a large
number of trucks parked in the desert."

A friend of Bubbles who was sharing dinner with us said, "Tell
them about your part."

Bubbles modestly tried to divert the conversation, but Dan and
I pressed him for the full story.

"Well, there were explosions near Bikaner. At first we thought
that war had started with Pakistan. Then the military issued an
order to evacuate the city. They said there was a problem at the
ammunition dump. My wife called to make sure I was safe and
leaving the city." Bubbles looked sheepish, "I said I was leaving the
city. But instead of driving away, I drove towards the explosions.
I was curious. When I arrived at the ammunition depot, a soldier
ran up to me and asked if I knew how to drive a truck. I said yes.
They weren't sure if it was sabotage or an accident, but some of the

explosives had detonated and were threatening to set off the entire fleet of trucks. They were desperate to move the trucks away from each other. As I drove one truck after another there were rounds of ammunition going off and rockets exploding. Many people in the area ran for their lives. I just kept going in to get more trucks."

Later we heard that Bubbles was named a hero of Bikaner. If the trucks had not been separated, Bikaner could have been heavily damaged.

The other reason Bubbles was so well recognized in Bikaner is because he had been put in prison.

"When they put me in jail, it was very embarrassing. My picture was on the front page of the paper," explained Bubbles. "Politics can be very heated in India. A close family friend was being threatened by the opposite political party for a stand he had taken. It became violent when they went to his home and threatened to burn it down with his wife and children inside. Calls to the police went unheeded, as the officers were in the other politician's pocket. When I heard what was happening I grabbed a hunting rifle and ran to his home. They fired the first shot and I shot back. I hit some of them. When the police arrived they put me in handcuffs but not those who had threatened my friend. I was only in jail a short time. But it was politics, not justice."

Dan and I instinctively liked Bubbles. Someone who stands by you when you are in trouble is the kind of friend you want. Later in the trip, we were going to need that kind of friend.

4 Head 'Em Up and Move 'Em Out

We spent much more time locating camels, training, and assembling gear than I had planned for. My prediction that our plan would fall apart was coming true. It took three weeks to get everything together (twenty-one days out of the allotted ninety-eight). We were more than a week behind schedule. Nevertheless, we felt we needed a few more weeks to work things out. I was getting nervous. Tibet seemed a long way away.

I didn't sleep well that night. I had looked forward to this adventure for two years, but now it was getting real. Sitting at the rooftop café that evening, Dan had charmed some of the hotel guests with stories of our preparations for the grand expedition. As Dan talked, I thought about the desert that was waiting for us with all of its unknowns. Living at the hotel, we'd forgotten about the desert. Even though our minds were filled with planning and preparation, crossing the desert was more a wish than a reality. We had become comfortable in our new environment, maybe a little too comfortable. We had room service, regular meals, and all the amenities. If we needed desert clothing we hired a tailor to custom-make shirts and pants. Camel feed was only a request away. Even veterinary services were just down the road. We could get help with anything we needed. It wouldn't be that way in the desert. I think Bubbles saw our adventurous spirit beginning to fade. That's when he said, "I think you are ready to leave. Let's look at your maps." It was the push that we needed.

Going over our maps, Bubbles suggested that we aim for one village in particular along the route. He had relatives there who would put us up for a few days. We accepted the invitation—assuming we could make it there.

The next day we woke at 4:00 A.M. to prepare for our departure. An early departure would help us avoid the dense traffic in town. Iqrar, our interpreter, arrived promptly, but Katea-ram was nowhere to be found. We asked Iqrar to try to find him while we packed our last bits of gear. Several hours later, still no Katea-ram. By then a crowd of reporters and television crews had arrived. Bubbles had alerted the media. He had us fitted with orange and green ceremonial turbans. Ceremonial turbans have a big poof that sticks out of the top. I looked like Priscilla, Queen of the Desert. Dan looked equally ridiculous but he was enjoying all the attention and flashing cameras.

Then a priest arrived to bless our adventure with a *puja* ceremony. He held out a bowl containing a *lingam*, a religious symbol on which we repeatedly dropped rice. We offered food to the gods, burned incense, held out our arms so that woven string bracelets could be tied to our wrists, and had our foreheads dabbed with a smudge of crimson paste for luck.

Next came a meeting with local dignitaries. After short speeches they added garland after garland of flower leis to our necks. I could barely see over the top of the flowers. We were now many hours behind schedule. In the media frenzy, Katea-ram showed up looking not the least hurried.

Dr. Bhadani arrived just in time. Tucked under his arm was the newly made banner for the *International Desert Animal Welfare Society of India*. He prominently draped the banner over Sam's packs. I glanced at the banner, flinching when I saw the recommendation to drink animal urine. That is when the newspaper photographers asked us to stand next to our camels. Dr. Bhadani slipped in next to us as the photographers clicked away.

Finally, each of us leading a camel, with Katea-ram in the lead, followed by Dan, Iqrar, and me in the back, we started down the street. Our caravan was under way.

I'm holding the banner given to us by Dr. Bhadani. The banner says there is scientific evidence that drinking animal urine increases how long a human will live. Dan and I did not test this theory.

In the Hindu religion, there are many gods. If there is a god of humor and mirth, we made him smile that day. Less than 100 yards from our start, still in view of the reporters and camera crews, Sam's pack started tilting to one side. We had gone to great trouble and expense to have custom camel panniers made. They looked like oversized versions of the doggie packs used by pooch-loving backpackers. The whole pack rotated on the girth straps, ending up underneath Sam like giant udders. Sam went wild. Trying to get rid of her awkward load she bucked and kicked. The crowd of well-wishers following us waded in to grab her. With fifty people trying to help, we rotated the pack back into position and tightened it. It was about then that people in the crowd started placing bets on how far we would make it.

Because of the media attention and all the preparations, we hadn't had a chance to eat, go to the bathroom, or get a drink of water—all those things parents make sure their children do before setting out on a trip. So I thought, *why not head back and take care of a few things?* Iqrar sensed my intention and said, "No. It is bad luck to go back when you have started out on a trip." I looked longingly at the hotel and turned away.

Baptism by Sewage

Our route out of Bikaner took us down busy streets with four jumpy camels at rush hour. We decided that leading the camels would be safer than riding. This was an understatement. Controlling 1,400 pounds of camel every time a vehicle went vrooming by was as relaxing as pogo-sticking across a mine field. That's when I had a near disaster. A large bus approached and Raika dug in. Like all good Indians, the bus driver leaned on his horn. *HOOOOOOOOOONNNNNKKKK!* Raika went berserk. Wild-eyed, she swung left and right. I held onto her reins to keep her from bolting into oncoming traffic. Yanking me about, she lost her footing. In slow motion I watched as she toppled over on her side into a ditch. The ditch was filled with raw sewage.

Raika panics at the approach of an oncoming bus and topples into a ditch of raw sewage.

A wave of sludge hit me. Rivulets of poop water ran down my
shirt and trousers. A foul piece of rotting vegetable matter stuck
to my crotch. Minutes before I had been a celebrity. Now I was a
leper. My hands and face were the only body parts that hadn't been
baptized. I wanted to pull the offending crotch lettuce off, but as
sweat trickled down my face, I wiped my brow and decided against
sacrificing a clean hand to the sludge. Katea-ram, who has no fear
of filth, happily wiped the slime from the front of my shirt with his
hands over my weak protests.

Holding Raika's reins I watched as rivulets of poop water ran down
my shirt and trousers. A foul piece of rotting vegetable matter stuck to
my crotch.

All I could do was walk. Crowds of well-wishers greeted us. They looked strangely at me as I smiled and greeted them in Hindi, "*Namaste.*" I'm sure they wanted to ask, "Why, sir, are you covered in sewage?" They probably thought it was a strange foreign custom.

It took a lifetime to get through town. No matter how tightly we cinched up the ropes, our loads repeatedly slipped off the camels. Traffic was a nightmare. As I looked at my previously *sahib* white shirt, now covered with excrement baking under the desert sun, I thought, *This is going to be a long day.* Well, it got longer yet.

Beat the Infidels

Just outside of town, my saddle started slipping again. Katea-ram looked at my saddle straps and uttered the one English phrase he was fluent in, "More tight." There was a big flat, clean open space just off the road where I could get my camel to kneel down to readjust the load. I thought our luck had changed. Any adjustments in town were done in congested and filthy areas. As I was getting things in order, a man rushed up to us shouting. Iqrar translated, "This is a holy site where the ground is used for prayer by the local Muslims." Hurriedly, we dragged our camels and their loads to another spot. The man was kind enough to invite me back to his house to take an open-air sitz bath. I was getting out of my filthy clothing and preparing to pour water from an earthenware crock over my body when Iqrar ran up to me.

"We need to go," he said.

"I'll be just a minute," I replied.

"No. We need to go *now!*"

"Give it a rest, I'll be there in a few minutes."

He ran back to the others.

Annoyed, I hurriedly washed and changed into fresh clothes.

When I got back, Katea-ram and Iqrar were already moving down the road.

Dan seeing my questioning look said, "See that post over there?"

I looked at an ordinary looking post, "Yeah."

"We tied our camels to it."

"So?"

"Turns out it has religious significance to the Muslims. A bloke saw what we did and went bonkers. He told Iqrar he's coming back with a gang. They are going to beat the infidel out of us."

Now I was moving. We jogged up the road with our camels in tow. For an hour we kept a fast pace, putting as much distance between us and the holy post and the gang as we could.

Heat shimmered off the blacktop. The air temperature was a baking 95° F. Dan, being British, prefers frigid drizzle or a nice damp fog. As the sun rose, so did Dan's temperature. Fighting nausea, he trudged along. Heat exhaustion isn't fun. Its close relative, heat stroke, is deadly. After several hours we decided to call it a day and pulled off into the dunes behind a truck stop.

Dan drank as much water as he could and slumped onto his ground pad. The sun having gone down, we hoped he'd cool down and shake the effects of heat exhaustion. I figured things couldn't get any worse. Wrong again. While eating a simple dinner, a hand-sized translucent spider ran up my pant leg. I'm not spiderphobic, but big spiders in my pants freak me out. In my panic, I spilled food over my only clean pants. Then it started to rain. As we struggled to get our tents set up, I thought, *This area of India has experienced a drought for three years and now it starts to rain?*

The next morning, I checked to make sure Dan was still alive. Unfortunately, he was. If he hadn't been, I thought I would have had a good excuse to end the trip.

Lighten Up

While researching the trip, I read that camels can carry heavy loads. For a Guiness Book World Record, an Australian camel rose from the ground carrying a 1,907 pound pack. If a camel could carry that much weight, I figured it would be no sweat for our camels to carry 300 pounds apiece, and since we had two pack camels, that meant we had room for 600 pounds of gear. That's a lot of luggage. In the planning stages, Dan and I considered bringing along a mess tent, tinned food, a shower tent, lounge chairs, and a folding potty. Dan imagined an expedition in the British Raj style of the 1800s. We ended up actually packing conservative 100 to 120 pound loads on each pack camel. This was well within their limits. Maybe within their limits, but not within the limits of our custom-made panniers. Our camel packs ripped apart along the seams after one day on the trail. Using the satellite phone, we called Bubbles back at the hotel. We needed to dump gear.

It took Bubbles all of twenty minutes—maybe less—to drive out to meet us. Originally, we had planned to travel twenty miles a day. On our first day we covered six miles. I can jog that far in an hour. As comedian Robin Williams put it, "Reality. What a concept!" What we'd planned theoretically was being replanned by reality. To speed up we needed to lighten up. We got rid of sleeping bags, clothing, spare boots, books, veterinary supplies, tools—half our gear was piled into the back of Bubbles's SUV to be shipped home.

At this point a TV crew showed up. They had looked for us all day, driving up and down the road on a motorcycle. They expected us to be a lot further along. Their camera was a standard Sony hand-held camcorder. We reenacted some of our camping experience for film and then gave them an interview.

As was to happen again and again during the trip, the reporters focused on Dan. It was as if I didn't exist. When they asked for a demonstration of our high tech Internet system, they wanted Dan to demonstrate. Setting up the system isn't hard. It requires connecting the solar charger and satellite phone to a Panasonic Toughbook computer, along with initiating the software uplink. The problem was that Dan didn't even know where the on button was on the computer. I was the tech head. They reluctantly watched me set up the equipment. The camera didn't start rolling until Dan sat in front of the screen. Dan assured me it had something to do with his good looks. "Yeah, right," I said. There was only one reason I could think of for making Dan the star of the expedition in the reporters' eyes. It was his accent. Speaking hoity-toity British, Dan sounds like a lord just off a foxhunt from the manor. Even when Dan doesn't have a clue what he is talking about, he sounds knowledgeable. I admit that I fell under the spell of his hypnotic accent at times. I don't know how we Americans got the nerve to kick the

British out of the U.S. All an English colonel had to say was, "Ye gads man, you don't mean you think you can govern the colonies all by yourselves, do you? I say, let's have a spot of tea and forget all this revolutionary nonsense." This would have left a lot of revolutionary minutemen scratching their heads in doubt. I think that's why we used guerrilla warfare tactics and shot redcoats from the bushes. That way we could run off before the British had a chance to use their accents on us.

Of course there wasn't a jealous bone in my body over Dan's celebrity status. OK, maybe an envious muscle or two. This annoyance was overshadowed by a more pressing concern—eating.

Don't go into the kitchen!

"Don't go into the kitchen!" warned Dan. We had ordered *chapattis*, a tortilla-like food, from a roadside stand. Dan, knowing my pickiness for cleanliness, thought it would be better if I didn't look. He was correct. Flies buzzed over the open food, birds perched on the mixing bowls, the dirt floor was littered with food waste. My first thought, *No way I'm eating here.* Then I studied the kitchen more carefully. The oven was built like a blast furnace. No pans were used for cooking the chapatti dough. It was plastered directly on the rock sides of the oven. Hot metal tongs were used to pick up the cooked dough, which was then dropped onto a plate. I made a judgment call. I'd use my own plate. The heat would kill anything in the dough. I ate chapattis.

Dan and I relied on local foods. We preferred buying directly from farmers rather than from food stands. Food stands were often swarming with flies and close to open sewers. In comparison, farmers' fields are quite clean. In the state of Rajasthan, farmers subsist on a vegetarian diet of dal beans, bazra (a grain used to make chapatti), saag (a variety of greens including spinach-like plants, mustard green, etc.), watermelons, and cucumbers. Occasionally sheep and chicken are eaten. When using meat, every part of the animal—including the internal organs—is eaten. The lungs are particularly interesting when you pull them out of a stew. There are lots of bones as well. Nothing goes to waste.

Cooking utensils in a farmer's home are simple. Pottery or brass pots are used to carry water from wells. Village women balancing pots of water on their heads as they make their way home are a common sight. A saucepan is reserved for making tea, a staple that includes milk from a camel, goat, cow, or water buffalo. We were partial to camel's milk in our tea. Then there are a few pots for boiling and a skillet for making dal and chapatti pancakes. Hands are used for eating. A single cup is dipped in a pot of drinking water and the water is poured into the mouth without touching it to your lips, a skill that takes some practice. Beginners often pour the contents down the front of a shirt. (Dan and I didn't drink local water without purification, but if we shared a bottle of purified water, we used the no-touch technique.)

Villagers collecting water at the local well. It takes a strong neck and good balance to carry the water home.

The fireplaces we were invited to cook on had two low mud walls for supporting pots, with the fire directly underneath. One day I noticed two boys playing in the sand near where our camels were tethered the night before. Then I realized they weren't playing. They were collecting camel poop. Dried camel dung is used for fires, as are other livestock droppings. We used water buffalo dung when wood was unavailable. It makes a smoky low-heat fire. We preferred wood with its hot, clean flame.

To clean up, villagers scour pots and pans with ashes or sand. This sand may also have the droppings of various animals mixed in. It's one reason we declined food unless it was hot from the skillet and dropped directly on our personal plates. We also cleaned with sand, but from a clean dune rather than a villager's front yard. Then, to be on the safe side, we rinsed our plates with heavily chlorinated water.

An Indian woman cooking tortilla-like chapattis. Two mud walls enclose the fire to her right. Occasionally, farmers would invite Dan and me to use their simple outdoor kitchens.

On the Trail

Our camels lined up caravan style, Iqrar pointed out the direction we were to follow. I kept a notebook with Hindi phrases that Iqrar taught us as we rode along. We needed to learn as much Hindi as we could. Iqrar would only stay with us for two weeks, and then we would be on our own asking directions, finding food and water, and requesting help.

Heading out across the Thar Desert with Iqrar in the lead. The landscape is dotted by spindly acacia trees which can be seen in the distance. On this particular day it was only 100° F.

Bubbles would have loved to travel with us, but obligations kept him in Bikaner. Still, he planned to meet with us periodically during the trip so we could share our stories. At one of our desert rendezvous he arrived in his SUV with a meal and hotel guests who had heard about our adventure. After brushing away a desert scorpion, we spread a tarp and unloaded the food. There were iced drinks, stew, ice, chapattis, ice cream, and ice. Dan and I got more pleasure from the ice than from a week at Disneyland. Ice cubes are short-lived diamonds—a desert luxury. During dinner we told stories about our comical mishaps and adventures.

Before leaving, Bubbles showed us how to build a refrigerator. He dug a hole in the sand and lined it with chunks of ice from his ice chest. Then he loaded the pit with bottled drinks and buried it. He waved good-bye and assured us the ice would last till morning.

The next morning I opened a bleary eye. Staring back at me were a lot of eyes—our audience. Whenever locals heard that we were in the vicinity, they would show up to wake us. This became a regular and annoying pattern. Crouched around our campsite, they'd watch everything with interest. I'd brush my teeth and they'd start chattering. Dan would open a meal from a tin and they'd mimic his movements. Dan would slip out of his shirt to change and the kids would yell, "Ghost." Of course Dan is as white as a porcelain doorknob. Most often, they pointed and laughed. We were desert celebrities. And like most celebrities hounded by the paparazzi, we found it tiring. Sometimes, Dan and I were a bit wicked in our responses. This was one of those mornings.

Having just finished packing up our camels, I turned dramatically towards our audience and stared at the space in front of me. Casually, I reached into the air. A coin appeared at my fingertips. A few more displays had our audience convinced I was a qualified wizard. The stage set, I leaped up. Grabbing a bamboo walking stick, I started swirling around doing my best imitation of an American Indian shaman's chant—Hayyaaa, hayaa, hayyaaaa, hayaaa…. The stick seemed to control me. Like a dowsing rod it had its own life force. It pulled, yanked, and jerked me around the campsite. Finally the stick came to rest on the ground. It scribed a circle in the sand. Solemnly, I indicated the spot to Dan who had watched amusedly up to this point. Nodding, he went to the spot and dug like a crazed gopher. When he pulled a piece of ice from the hole and held it towards the sky, there were, "Ohs," "Ahs," and "Ooohs," all around. The onlookers watched in amazement as Dan pulled chunk after chunk of ice from the pit. Unaware of Bubbles's late-night delivery, the audience saw us performing a miracle in the desert. Just prior to leaving, I went through the same gyrations and indicated another spot in the sand to our audience. Then we mounted our camels and rode off. I wonder how long they dug after our departure.

True to his word, Katea-ram refused to ride a camel. Every morning he'd take one of the pack camel's reins and set the pace with the rest of us following. Dan, Iqrar, and I preferred to ride. Swaying along on the camels, Dan and I discussed the day's plans.

"Mate, 'dya think Iqrar or Katea-ram have any idea where we are?" asked Dan.

"I think Iqrar knows some of the area," I replied. "But he's lost half of the time. You know how he says, 'No problem.' I think that's when we need to worry the most. And Katea-ram has never been this far from his home."

Finding our way shouldn't have been a concern. Dan and I are experienced navigators. Plus, we had all the high tech toys: a global positioning unit (GPS), compasses, and incredibly detailed British air survey maps. There was a hitch, though. In his haste to get maps, Dan had not checked to make sure he was sent the correct maps. Our maps covered an area far north of our route. Without maps, the GPS and compass were worthless. They could do little more than point out north, east, south, and west. So we bought a simple Indian road map to keep us on course.

Looking at our cheap road map, I asked, "Dan, why don't we use the train tracks to keep us on track? We follow the rail lines when they are going in our general direction. That way we avoid roads and traffic problems. Train tracks are straightforward and don't have all the confusing intersections we find on the dirt tracks."

"What about the trains?" asked Dan. "The camels go crazy

when they see a bicycle, what do you think they will do when a train goes by?"

"We keep an eye on the horizon," I said. "You can see the smoke put out by the train from a long way off. If we see a train coming we dismount and lead the camels away from the tracks. There aren't going to be that many trains every day anyway."

"Sounds like a plan."

So a fifty-cent road atlas, which showed train tracks, major roads, big towns, and some villages became our guide.

Desert Opera

That night there was entertainment. I chose a sand dune for my sleeping spot. Dan picked an adjacent mound. It was a dripping-sweat hot night. Everyone was stripped to their underwear, lying in the open. That's when we heard a tinkling, jingling, jangling. I rolled over and propped myself on one arm to see where the music was coming from. Over a moonlit rise appeared a flock of goats, bells around their necks. They moved through our campsite, scavenging for food scraps, sniffing our packs, and bleating at the camels. Then a taller silhouette appeared on the dune—the goats' owner. As he trudged down the sandy slope, he suddenly stopped. He couldn't have been more surprised if he had discovered a beached Amazonian albino river dolphin. Dan's white skin seemed to glow in the moonlight. The goatherd stared. Dan casually said, *"Namaste"* (Hello). There was no response. Dan made more attempts at conversation, *"Kyaa haal hay?"* (How are you doing?). Still no response. The goatherd simply stood looking at Dan. It was becoming increasingly awkward. After several minutes Dan politely asked the goatherd to continue on his way. He didn't move. Then Dan became not so polite. Still the goatherd stood there. I was doubled up with laughter.

"Whot' the bloody heck am I supposed to do?" asked Dan looking in my direction. "I'm not going to sleep with this twit standing over me."

My reply was a snurfled laugh.

"Get stuffed," huffed Dan. "You're a lot of help."

Then the goatherd and I got a surprise. Two hundred and forty pound Dan stood up, dressed only in his underwear, spread his arms against the backdrop of a star-lit sky, and sang a piece from an opera. Dan has trained in the theater arts. The goatherd watched transfixed. On the last note of his operetta, Dan sat down, frustrated.

"The man has less brains than his goats," said Dan. "You'd think the sight of a near-naked foreigner singing an opera on a sand dune at night would drive off any sane person."

The goatherd, still staring, seemed to consider what had just happened. Coming to a decision, he shifted his herding stick under his arm, slowly raised his hands, and clapped politely. Then he and his goats disappeared into the night.

A lone goat herder appeared over the rise silhouetted by the moon. He was in for a surprise.

The Rat Temple

It took us three days to reach the town of Deshnok. This was three times longer than I'd planned. We had traveled only 20 miles. Deshnok has a temple famous throughout India. Tying our camels to a hitching tree and leaving Katea-ram and Iqrar to watch over them, Dan and I entered the temple.

Thousands of beady eyes watched us. Coarse black hair, slithering tails—wall-to-wall rats. When you enter the rat temple at Deshnok, you might miss the intricate carvings of elephants, cobras, ibis, and rats covering the temple walls. The real rats catch your eye. Here rats are worshipped as reincarnated deities. Gods in rodent bodies. These rats, or *cabbi* as they are referred to by holy men, don't have to worry about a Terminix Pest Control truck in the neighborhood. They may be the most pampered rats on the planet. Bowls of milk two feet across were surrounded by squirming bodies. Rats perched on the rim of the bowls like birds around birdbaths and sipped the milk. Other rats nibbled grain scattered by worshippers on the marble floor. Nets strung from the roof kept birds of prey from snatching a holy snack.

The temple at Deshnok was occupied by thousands of rats. These holy rats, known as *cabbi,* are worshipped. Bowls of milk and grain scattered on the floor make sure that no rat goes hungry.

This is Rat Club Med. The holy rodents ran to and fro in front of tourists, hopped over feet, or lounged on the floor napping on their backs, four feet in the air. You expected to see mini-soda cans in their paws and little beach umbrellas providing shade. They knew they were safe in their shrine.

You had to take your shoes off to enter the temple. Hygiene-wise this made me nervous. Thoughts of bubonic plague, rabies, all kinds of ratty diseases played through my mind. Fortunately, you could leave your socks on. Afterwards I trashed my socks. Rat urine is a potent perfume. Washing my socks many times didn't remove the smell, or maybe the odor was in my imagination. Even Indian women visiting the temple were nervous, hopping from foot to foot when a curious rat ran under their skirts.

At the temple, we walked through corridors from left to right. This is supposed to bring luck. We were looking for a white rat. To see one brings even more luck.

What with all the newspaper accounts and television coverage, everyone in Deshnok knew we were the foreigners riding camels across India. People came up to us in the temple to wish us luck, as did the rats.

Holy rats weren't the only exotic animals we saw in India. Riding across the desert I spotted a creature with its front legs propped against a thorn tree straining to reach leaves on the upper branches. It looked like a horse from the Jurassic, a long-legged beast with a neck almost as thick as its buff, muscled body. These are *nilgai*. The nilgai roam wild across the desert. Part of their freedom is due to their name. Nilgai means blue bull. In the Hindu religion, the bull is sacred, so the name gives religious protection to the animal—if you are Hindu. Hindus worship bulls. Actually, the nilgai is not a bull. It is related to the antelope. The name was given to the creature by Muslims. Putting the word "bull" into the animal's name makes Hindus reluctant to hunt nilgai. There is a fear of angering the gods. In the Muslim religion, there is no problem with putting nilgai on the dinner table. In a nation hungry for protein, at least the nilgai doesn't have everyone looking at him as a source of Blue Bull Burgers.

A nilgai, also known as a blue bull.

Sandstorm

Keeping an eye on the terrain for animals wasn't the only thing to watch out for. Not many days into the trip, I looked over my shoulder and noted a dark cloud coming our way.

"Looks like we are in for some more rain," I said pointing at the cloud.

Iqrar shook his head. "Do you see the line where the darkness meets the sky?"

I looked and noted that the cloud seemed to start from ground level and then cut off high in the sky. "Strange looking cloud."

"It is not a cloud. It is a desert sandstorm," he said. "We must find shelter."

The camels sensed it coming. They started twitching and skittering about. Controlling them was difficult. In the movie, *The Mummy*, a demonic sandstorm threatens the main characters. They race ahead of the storm desperately seeking refuge. Just as the storm is about to overtake them, they gallop into an ancient ruin where the walls break the fury of the storm. Something similar happened to us. The storm moved incredibly fast. A wall of airborne sand, maybe 300 feet high, avalanched towards us. Fortunately, we were on the outskirts of a village. The villagers motioned us to a schoolyard surrounded by a solid wall. We scrambled off our mounts and led them into the courtyard. Then the storm hit. Even with a wall between the storm and us, fierce sand devils scoured the enclosure. In the blink of an eye, my eyes were filled with grit. It was like stumbling around in a sand-blasting machine as we clumsily tied our camels to a few spindly trees. Desert veterans, they hunkered down to ride out the storm.

At this point Dan was fall-down sick. His body was having a tough time adjusting to the heat. I set up his tent in an open hallway of the school as sand swirled and eddied across the stone floor. By the time I'd gotten him sheltered inside his tent, watered, and medicated, I was beat. Setting up my own tent seemed to be too much of a chore. I unrolled my ground pad, said, "Forget the tent," and wrapped my turban around my face to keep the sand out of my mouth and dropped off to sleep.

In the morning I woke with sand in everything. I had sand in my ears and nostrils. My mouth felt like I had eaten a dune cupcake. My bellybutton had disappeared, filled in during the night. Even my underwear and my…well you get the idea.

Iqrar and Katea-ram were already up.

"Katea-ram thinks you should bargain with the villagers," said Iqrar.

"What do they have that we need?" I asked as I dug sand out of my ears.

Iqrar looked at our panniers heaped on the ground and partially buried.

"Katea-ram thinks you should buy Indian camel packs," Iqrar pointed to where Katea-ram was talking with a group from the village. "He's asking if anyone has packs for sale."

"But we've got camel packs," I retorted feeling defensive. "We went to a lot of trouble to get those panniers made. We had to find military-grade canvas, heavy thread, nylon straps, and metal rivets."

About this time, Dan stuck his head out of his tent, "I think

Katea-ram is right. Those packs were supposed to be bombproof. They just look bombed."

Staring at the packs, I reluctantly agreed. Here we were, only days into the trip and the pack seams were splitting, straps had ripped off, and there were holes where the camels had rubbed up against thorny trees.

"Plus, the bloody things keep falling off," said Dan. "If I hear Katea-ram say 'More tight,' one more time I'm going to... ."

I interrupted, "Why didn't Katea-ram suggest these camel packs when we were in Bikaner running around looking for a seamstress and all the supplies?"

"I think he wants us to learn from our mistakes," said Dan. "Remember the resin we bought because we thought it was some kind of medicine? He stood there and watched us buy it. It didn't have anything to do with camels."

Iqrar waved for us to come over to the circle where the villagers were gathered.

Katea-ram was inspecting something lying on the ground. It looked like a jumbo doormat. Iqrar translated.

"These are what Indian camel men use," said Iqrar. "It's a bag made out of goat hair. Try lifting one."

I grabbed the edge of the bag and hoisted it, "The darn thing is heavy. Must weigh 20 pounds."

Katea-ram gave us a demonstration. He loaded the bag and folded over the opening. Then he hoisted it over a camel saddle. It slopped over each side like a giant tamale. Katea-ram lashed the bag to the saddle. With a big superior smile, he said, "No more tight," tugging at the ropes.

We bought two bags. Thrown into the deal were a pencil-sized needle and some tough goat hair thread for repairs.

These bags eliminated our slippage problems. They also made Katea-ram happy. If there was one thing that put a smile on his face it was: Katea-ram is right; Dan and Jim are wrong.

Katea-ram's attitude was beginning to irritate Dan. Dan would concede that Katea-ram knew more about camels, but knots and ropes are something Dan takes great pride in. As a professional climbing guide who has led ascents in Nepal, Europe, and the U.S., Dan is a knot encyclopedia. Yet, Katea-ram would look at Dan's knots, undo them, and then tie them the "right" way. Purchasing the goat hair bags meant Katea-ram had a whole new series of lashings and knots to teach us. I think this made Dan stubbornly decide that he would do something that Katea-ram had said a foreigner was incapable of.

Sam showing off her new camel pack. These packs were made from goat hair and were so tough they could be rubbed against a thorn tree without damaging the material.

Camel Milk

Katea-ram was convinced that we would not be able to milk a camel. One of our camels, GB, was still producing milk when we bought her.

"Katea-ram says it will be too dangerous for an inexperienced person to milk a camel," translated Iqrar.

"How hard can it be to milk a camel?" retorted Dan. "It's got to be pretty much the same as a cow."

"It takes much practice," said Iqrar. "First, you milk a sheep, then a goat, after that a cow. With much practice you might milk a camel. It will take several weeks."

"Bloody nonsense," said Dan.

As the voice of reason, I said, "Dan, Iqrar may be right. They can kick hard enough to knock you into next week. And you and GB aren't on the best of terms. How many times has she bitten you?"

"She can be a dodgy beast," said Dan.

"Think about it," I said.

Dan thought about it and came up with a plan. First we hobbled GB's front legs. Then we tied a rope to each rear leg. I held one of the rear leg ropes far enough away to keep from being kicked. We convinced a reluctant Iqrar to hold the other rope. Earlier in the day he had been thrown by Humper and was still a little camel-shy. Dan cleaned GB's udders with a pan of water, as it is done in a village. Carefully grasping GB's teats, he started the milking process. Squirt, squirt, into the pan it went. Katea-ram did not look pleased that GB just stood there. As soon as Dan was done, he turned and offered Katea-ram some fresh camel milk for his tea. I don't doubt that Dan took great pleasure in making this offer.

Camel Talk III

"You carried milk in your body?" asked Sam.

"Yes," said GB.

"But that means you had a baby not long ago," said Sam. "The milk would have been for your baby."

"I did."

"But where is the baby?"

"Nowhere. Everywhere. Camels don't decide where their children live. The last food givers took her. My baby struggled and cried as they led her away. I tried to break loose but they had me hobbled and tied to a tree. Later I tried to follow, but her scent disappeared in the hot desert air."

"I'm sorry."

"Step on their feet," said Raika.

"What?"

"Step on their feet," repeated Raika. "That's what I do to the thin food giver. When I walk behind him, I step on his heels. He doesn't like it at all."

"You are asking for a beating," said GB.

"These food givers don't beat," said Raika. "They are too weak. Step on their feet. It will make you feel better. Or you could throw them off your back like dim-witted Humper did."

"Accident, accident," whined Humper. "I heard a sound and jumped off the ground. If you throw they give you a blow."

"When that little two-leg rolled off your back, he fell right in front of me," said Raika. "I tried to dislodge mine but the thin food giver isn't as careless. He always holds on to the saddle with one hand."

Black Buck Reserve

A few days later, I did something Dan calls a Wally—a dumb thing. In the desert, you need to drink six to eight liters of water a day to stay healthy. I drank three liters of water that day. We were riding through a black buck reserve, and I was more intent on spotting the antelope-like animal with spiraling horns than drinking water. Black bucks are one of the fastest land animals and can get up to 50 mph (cheetahs sprint at 70 mph). By the time we made camp I was severely dehydrated, my brain and stomach took turns doing somersaults. While unloading, hobbling, and feeding the camels, I felt faint. The desert rolled under my feet like a ship at sea. Even though I stood on solid ground, I felt seasick. Just before my stomach mutinied, I sank to the ground. Dan poured a rehydration packet into a liter of water and insisted I drink it. Laying on the ground trying not to vomit, I feebly swatted at a swarm of flies that had taken an interest in me. Then the breeze shifted. A horrible stench wafted over me. Unfortunately, we had picked a spot fifty feet from a decomposing water buffalo carcass. I fell asleep, or passed out depending on how you define it, with the cloying smell of decaying flesh in my nostrils and flies buzzing in my ears.

Desert Survival

When the thermometer hits 100° F, people without water die within a couple of days. At such high temperatures, the desert traveler needs at least a gallon of water a day. If you conserve energy and stay in the shade, every gallon of water is equal to another day of life. If you decide to move, doing so at night is a good choice. A healthy person could make about twenty miles on a gallon of water in the cooler night air. If you travel in the daytime heat, two to three times as much water is needed.

The reason you need so much water is that your body works best in a narrow temperature range around 98.6° F. This is the temperature at which your body functions best. As your temperature rises, as can happen in the desert, you start having problems. If your temperature reaches 103° F you will only survive for a short time. Water helps to keep your temperature down. When water evaporates it takes heat with it. The sweat that forms on your skin is what keeps you from overheating. If you take a canteen of water and a desert water bag (a type of canteen made out of tightly woven canvas, which allows the bag to sweat) and placed both water containers in the sun, the water in the solid canteen could reach 110° F while the desert bag would be 70° F. Evaporation keeps the desert bag 40° cooler than the canteen, just as the sweat from your body keeps you cool. Of course the desert bag eventually dries up unless you replenish the water.

The Fortress

It took us ten days to make it to the village Bubbles had pointed out on the map. When we arrived we were in for a surprise. At the village we learned that Bubbles was descended from a line of maharajas, the kings of India. We would be staying at his country home. His country home turned out to be a cross between a castle and a fort. It had turrets, fortress walls, cisterns, gun ports, stables, and living quarters. Portions of the fortress were over 200 years old. In many ways, it was like staying at an archaeological site.

The fortress was in a state of decay. Some surrounding walls were crumbling into the desert sands. Bats occupied dark corridors; paint flaked from the walls; and the ceilings were covered by water stains from leaks. The ceilings of the rooms and corridors were studded with metal rings. These rings once supported rods from which hung short colorful curtains. Servants at opposite ends of a room or corridor held ropes that were pulled to make the curtains fan the area below. Bright-hued curtains of royal red, purple, and yellow would have made the fortress look like the brightly colored peacocks that now perched on the walls. Towers of the fortress were dotted with slots, allowing defenders to fire flintlock guns at an approaching enemy. There was also a defense against a strange warfare tactic. When storming a fortress, the enemy would bring large desert lizards, *godi*. They tied ropes to these three-foot-long lizards and tossed them over the fortress walls. These lizards cling so tightly that they can support 200 pounds. The attackers would

then climb the ropes while the lizards clung to the walls like living grappling hooks. To prevent a large group of lizard-toting men
from massing at the base of the fortress wall, there was another
type of slot cut in the rock work. This slot pointed down towards
the base of the fortress wall like a gutter spout. If any lizard-toting
soldier made it to the base of the castle wall, the defenders poured
boiling water through the slots to shower the men and lizards.

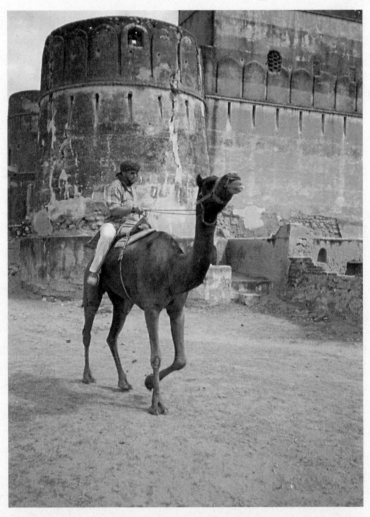

Dan rides GB outside the fortress walls. Note the gun port notches
in the wall. The downward pointing slots allowed defenders to pour
boiling liquid on attackers at the base of the wall.

On our arrival, chairs were arranged in the courtyard where the men waited to greet us. Many were dressed in traditional long white shirts and *dhoti*, loose pants that are wrapped around the waist from a single sheet of fabric. Their jet-black hair was slicked back. We were introduced to brothers, uncles, cousins, and friends of Bubbles's family. As we talked, I detected a big difference between Bubbles and his relatives. When I asked Bubbles what he would do if he could go on any great adventure, he immediately replied that he would go to Africa to hunt big game. He was filled with ideas. The men in the village, when asked, "Where would you travel to if you could?" replied, "Why?"

On further probing one gentleman said, "I would only go to America if I could get a good job." He leaned forward and asked, "Do you have cows in the streets?" "Could I get a job on a farm?" Farming is the only skill they knew here. From our conversation, we found that they lived for one thing—the harvest. It rules their lives. And after three years of drought they were worried. Water is life.

Water is captured during the short rainy season. This supply then has to last the rest of the year for cooking, drinking by both humans and animals, and washing. The water at the castle was held in five rock-walled cisterns buried in the ground. They were similar to the cisterns we saw at smaller farms in the desert. An area ten to twenty feet in diameter around the cistern was cleared and the soil sloped funnel-like towards an opening in the top of the buried tank. To increase the size of the catchment area, upper roof drains led down to the tanks. To get a drink, we lowered a bucket into the underground reservoir. The U.S., which is beginning to experience shortages, might consider the advantage of having cisterns to collect rainwater. Even if rainwater were only used for gardens and general cleaning, it would make efficient use of a dwindling resource.

Women were noticeably absent from our meeting. Occasionally, we saw them peeking at us from behind upper parapets. Veils covered their faces. The ancient custom of women hiding their faces in the presence of strange men was a common sight in villages. While this custom is dying out in the big cities, even Bubbles's wife, a modern Indian woman, covers her face when visiting the village as a sign of respect for rural traditions. In the old days, maybe fifty years ago, the upper terraces of the castle were divided into two areas—one for men and another for women. Unless you were family, men and women did not mix. While the rules are not as strict as in old India, there is still a strong division between men and women.

While Dan and I were staying at the Fortress, Bubbles's family drove out from Bikaner to visit with his relatives who live there. Bubbles is the tall dark-haired man, second from the left, holding his daughter. His wife is seated in the front row, second from right, wearing the flowered sari. Normally the women would have remained veiled, but they removed their veils for this photo.

A flickering pattern on one turret wall told us it was dinner-time. The light came from an outdoor fire where the women prepared the evening meal. Dinner included dense desert chapatti. "Bet you can only eat one" is the slogan. There was also *papadam*, a potato-chip thin tortilla with hot peppers that give it a bite. This was followed by potatoes, dal beans, a spicy yellow stew, and watermelon. Our shrunken stomachs swelled with all the food. The men brought down the meal. The women ate separately later.

In a display of hospitality that humbled Dan and me, the family cleared out one room so that we had a place to stay. Pictures of past maharajas lined the walls. There were candles for power blackouts. A walk-through window led to a balcony that looked out on a temple across the road. The temple looked old, but there was a modern addition. An ugly erector set-like mast protruded from the temple dome. At first I thought it was a radio tower. Then I noticed the large loudspeaker at the top. It was aimed at our room.

Rock With the Gods

It is said that you can see the Great Wall of China from outer space. Astronauts confirm that lights from major U.S. cities are visible from the space shuttle. And, while I've never been there, I'm sure you can hear India from Pluto. The rock concert-sized loudspeaker aimed at our room powered up at 6:00 P.M. Like barking dogs, other loudspeakers came on across the village. It was a volume competition. I'm sure that these temple DJs could talk ohms, amps, and decibels with any Western techno-weenie. Dan and I tried to muffle the sound by covering our heads with pillows. It was like being at an Ozzy Osbourne concert and lying in front of the speakers. Both of us were thinking, *It will stop by seven.* Then, *It will stop by eight.* Then, *It will stop by nine.* Then, *It will stop by*…around midnight Dan suggested we climb over the wall and clip the loudspeaker wires. It lasted till six the next morning.

Most of the religious music was taped, playing in an endless loop. There's a particular female voice that still haunts me. At one point she repeated "Ram-Ram-Ram" endlessly. Another feed somewhere in the village was live. I was sure the person chanting would get laryngitis before the end of the evening, but no such luck. The man had vocal chords of steel. Bubbles's relatives agreed that this religious noise is annoying. Annoying! More like insanity inducing. The music went on every night we were there. We were told that the religious think the gods are listening. If this is true, I think the gods had pillows over their heads as well.

The Camel-Dancing Teacher

Riding our camels was as relaxing as juggling scorpions. We were still beginners when it came to reading our camels' moods and controlling them. At the castle, we discovered someone who we thought might help us with our difficult beasts.

Jagmal had a wrinkled face, thin legs, and a stooped 72-year-old body. Jagmal was a camel-dancing instructor. He traveled from village to village teaching camels to dance. A dancing camel lifts its feet in time to music and will respond to the slightest command from its master. We bargained with him to give us several days of camel riding lessons.

When Jagmal mounted Raika, she showed her naughty side. She swirled and backed into walls. Jagmal ordered the gates of the fort opened and he took off at a mad gallop. Frail-looking Jagmal stuck to her back like a desert burr. An hour later, he returned. Raika looked like she had run a marathon. Over the next couple of days, Jagmal had Dan and I galloping across sand tracks. We weaved through waving grain stalks, patches of watermelon, and dal bean fields. At a camel lope, we passed mud-walled huts, the occasional water buffalo, and villagers calling out the greeting "Ram-Ram." Riding a cantering camel for several hours left me more tired than if I'd gone for a run on my own. Jagmal took no pity. Dan and I were pushed back on our camels for more riding. Jagmal said, "It takes thirty days to train a dancing camel. If we had the time, I could train your camels to dance across India." We explained to Jagmal that we would be satisfied with a camel that stopped and started on command.

Dan made consistent progress on GB. I think Dan's happiest day was when GB responded to his commands to kneel. Up to this point, Dan had required Katea-ram's assistance to get GB to go down. Raika, on the other hand, was schizophrenic. One moment she would nuzzle my ear like we were best friends. The next, she bit me full on in the chest. She challenged authority. Even Jagmal found her difficult. Humper and Sam, being pack camels, were excused from the riding lessons and watched with interest from the sidelines.

Camel Talk IV

While Raika was led away to the other side of the compound, Sam and Humper nibbled grain from their food mat.

"Did you see that cobra on the trail yesterday?" asked Sam. "It gave me such a scare, I thought I would jump over my own shadow. The big food giver on GB's back seemed excited, but not with fear. I thought he might follow the snake into the bushes."

"Cobras, cobras, give them space, otherwise they bite your face," recited Humper.

"It's a wise saying," agreed Sam. "There was a camel in our village who was eating leaves from a pile of branches on the ground. The wind must have blown the wrong way. He did not smell the snake hiding in the pile. The cobra sank its fangs into the camel's nose. In the time it takes a dung beetle to dig a hole, this camel's nose grew to the size of a melon. His hurt could be heard far into the desert. That night he died."

Humper moaned.

"Don't worry about cobras, we have something worse," said Sam inclining her head towards Raika who was nipping at a two-leg. "How many times has she pushed us away from the water so she could drink first, or snapped at us for eating before she had finished, or kicked for no reason?"

"Raika, Raika, give her space, otherwise she bite your face," said Humper.

Sam snorted. "You're right. She has a cobra's soul."

Suddenly a roaring sound came from Raika. The two keepers struggled to hold a plastic bottle to her mouth. A pink liquid dribbled down her lips.

Watching the two keepers forcing the pink water into Raika's mouth, Humper said distastefully, "Bitter pink, bitter pink, the bad water they make us drink."

"If I was as dry as sand I would not willingly drink that pink water," said Sam. "It is so foul, the ticks drop from my neck and belly after I have been made to swallow it."

A creaking gate caught their attention. An old man carrying a saddle and a thin bamboo rod entered the courtyard.

"Old keeper with a stick, I wonder which camel he will hit," chanted Humper.

"He has the smell and sound of one who has been with camels a long time," whispered Sam. "He carries a stinging stick but GB says he does not hit hard with it. The stick in his hand says listen. Even our new food givers learn from him. He has taught the big food giver to make the kneeling command not only with his mouth but with his body as well."

The old man fit a riding saddle on Raika's back.

"Raika won't be happy," said Sam. "She doesn't like the old keeper. He can force her to do his bidding."

Jagmal grips Humper's lips to keep her mouth open while Katea-ram pours a deworming solution in. The deworming solution had the added benefit of ridding the camels of the ticks that infested their bodies.

The Last Supper

The training ended too soon and we prepared to continue on. This time we wouldn't have the support of Iqrar or Katea-ram. They had promised to stay with us for two weeks. Going so far from home made them uncomfortable. In the morning they would return by bus to Bikaner. That night we invited Katea-ram to eat with us. Previously at the castle, he had eaten separately. This was because of his caste.

In India, people are born into a system that assigns them a caste. Supposedly, your past lives determine your caste or position in your present life. If you lived a wholesome life in your previous life, you rise in the caste system. Live an evil life and you come back as the lowest of the castes or maybe even as a tsetse fly. There are five castes in India. The *Brahmins* are the highest and represent the intellectuals and priests. *Kshatriyas* are the rulers and warriors. *Vaishyas* are the farmers and merchants. *Shudras* are the servants. *Harijans* or untouchables are the lowest class. In the United States we have caste systems, but they are assigned based on different criteria. Think about how a university educated Ph.D. is viewed as more important than someone with an elementary school education. Or money is another form of a caste system. People with lots of money are treated differently than the poor. In India, you inherit your caste from your parents. If your parents are low caste, you are low caste, and there's nothing you can do about it. While modern Indians say the caste system is no longer in effect, we still saw evidence of it. For example, Katea-ram, an untouchable, felt uncomfortable eating with us while at the castle. So he took his meals separately.

While Dan and I couldn't care less about castes, we were sensitive to the customs of the people we were traveling among. But on our last night, we asked Bubble's relatives if it would be O.K. if Katea-ram dined with us. Since Dan and I are *Malecha* (foreigners outside the caste system) it seemed a reasonable request. Katea-ram was so moved by the gesture that he touched our legs and bowed to our feet. When we returned this "sign of respect," tears came to his eyes and ours as well.

While there were times when we wanted to wring his neck, Katea-ram fully supported our adventure. Even when things were tough he had a ready smile and twinkle in his eye. He's also one of the toughest people I have known. Our trip was the furthest he'd ever been from his home in Bikaner. He walked 140 kilometers in ill-fitting flip-flops, that flopped apart by the end of the journey. He also didn't get the banana lassies he was fond of in Bikaner. On the road the best he could do for some meals was tea. If that isn't convincing toughness, consider that he has sired fifteen children, nine of whom are still alive. Having dinner together seemed a fitting way to end an adventure that he would talk about for the rest of his life.

As we ate dinner we shared superstitions.

"In India, walking under a ladder or crossing the path of a black cat is bad luck," said Iqrar.

"It's the same in England and America," said Dan.

"It is also not wise to follow a woman carrying an empty pot," added Iqrar.

"That's probably because she might ask you to carry it back when it is full," quipped Dan.

"Mothers also paint black under the eyes of young children," said Iqrar. "This protects the child from illness and the evil eye of the jealous."

"I wondered why all the little kids wore mascara," I said.

That night I used our satellite system to check email. One email was particularly disturbing. My wife forwarded a bulletin from the U.S. State Department that said Maoist rebels were threatening to kill U.S. citizens in Nepal. Reacting to this threat, a travel warning had been issued. The State Department recommended that U.S. tourists leave or avoid Nepal. Road travel outside the Kathmandu Valley was considered dangerous. Among other events, bomb blasts at an American compound resulted in the Peace Corps's suspending operations in Nepal and the voluntary evacuation of nonessential U.S. personnel. Any U.S. citizens in Nepal were cautioned to keep a low profile. Low profile? How do you do that on a camel? Our original plan was to cross Nepal. In light of the Maoist threat, we considered a change in plans. We were too big a target.

That wasn't the least of our problems. We'd been warned by camel experts that the chances of two camel novices making it across India, let alone into and through Nepal, were slim.

"Dan," I said, "I think making it to Tibet isn't realistic. I talked with Iqrar last night and he said he thought we'd be lucky to make it to Agra in India."

"Let's play it by ear," said Dan.

The next morning we said goodbye to Iqrar and Katea-ram as they boarded a bus to return to Bikaner. Then Dan and I headed off into the desert on our own.

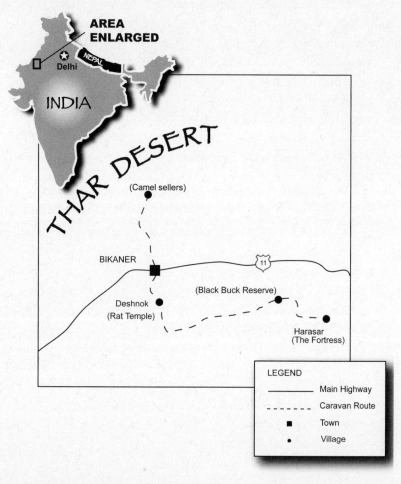

Katea-ram and Iqrar came with us from Bikaner to the Fortress. From then on we would be on our own.

On the Trail On Our Own

Leaving behind our camel expert and interpreter, you'd think things would have been harder. In many ways it was easier. Dan and I were in agreement on issues that had to do with cleanliness, camel care, when to stop, and where to camp. Completely in charge of the camels, we felt like two teens with the keys to the car. We were the masters of the road. Until two hours later.

After a rest break, I tried to mount a cantankerous Raika. Now that we no longer had Katea-ram and Iqrar to lead our pack camels, Dan and I had to control two camels each. As Raika swirled, I tried to avoid getting tangled in the lead line attached to Sam.

"Noooo!" I yelled.

"What?" asked Dan.

I slid to the ground off Raika. "Sam's reins got tangled in Raika's saddle. She's got a broken nose peg." Blood dribbled from Sam's nose where the peg had snapped off.

A broken nose peg was our biggest fear. We graphically remembered watching a crowd of experienced Indian camel nose-peggers struggle with the procedure. Now two beginners would have to repeat the operation from memory.

Dan was promoted to camel doctor. I got to be the nurse. This meant I had to restrain the patient. To hold her head steady, I got my best wrestler's half-nelson grip around her neck. In our first attempt at jamming a peg up Sam's nose, she casually picked me off the ground and slammed me on my back. I got bruised ribs.

Humans 0, Sam 1. We then enlisted the help of four village boys to hold her head. This resulted in four boys being tossed about. Humans 0, Sam 2. That's when we hired a bemused village elder. He fashioned a halter out of a car tire and tied it over Sam's head. Then he slipped a hefty tree branch into the halter, and had two people stand on the branch to secure Sam's head to the ground. The peg was inserted with a lot of camel roaring. Humans 1, Sam 2.

In the next few days, Dan and I pushed the limits of our Hindi language skills. That's because we were on a breaking spree. We broke nose pegs, *bali doris* (a woven line to the reins), a saddle, and one human shoe. To make repairs we needed help from the local villagers. This meant we had to speak Hindi. No one out here in rural India spoke English. To explain some of our more complex requirements, I brought out my notebook and pencil and drew diagrams of what we needed. A picture is worth a thousand words.

The villagers were helpful. We crouched down with them while they taught us how to weave the reins that are attached to nose pegs, a metal worker followed our diagram to pound out a metal sleeve to splint a broken saddle bar, and everyone wanted to show us better ways to pack our camels. At this point though, we declined camel-packing help. Dan, with all his rope working skills, had been experimenting. He'd come up with a simple, secure system, better than the traditional one taught to us by Katea-ram. We knew it was good. Humper was our harshest critic. Humper spooked at slamming gates, loud noises, and insect bites. In these camel fits she did her best to throw off her pack.

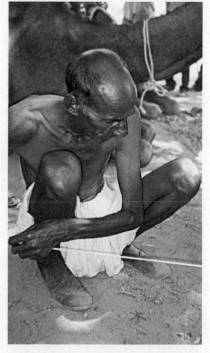

A villager shows us how to weave a *bali doris*, the line that attaches a camel's nose peg to the reins.

When the gear was still in place after one of Humper's bucking-bronco tests we felt confident in our packing ability.

In addition to being helpful, the local farmers were generous. Shaking their heads when we offered to pay, they brought us gifts of watermelons and giant cucumbers. A watermelon was a desert treat. Hacking the fruit in half we spooned out the greenish melon flesh and slurped up the liquid. Half the contents of these melons are seeds. Dan spits them out. I decided the seeds added to the roughage in my diet and swallowed them. The camels loved the rinds.

One of our least favorite things in the desert was something the locals called "scorpion plant." Dan and I gave it names like the devil's velcro, cat's claws, and misery. This plant has tiny burrs that stick to everything: pants, ropes, saddles, blankets, flesh, and even smooth plastic ground sheets. Attempts at brushing off the burrs resulted in getting pricked by their bee-sting thin needles. We tried to choose campsites away from this vicious weed. I swear the plant leaped across any open space to attack us. Every morning I went through a burr removal ritual. Donning a pair of leather gloves I brushed myself, then my gear, and finally my camels. I still managed to get "bitten" by these burrs. The only way to remove the spines from skin was to let them fester into pop-able pimples. I believe Hades is landscaped with this plant. If you are a bad person the devil asks you to tend his garden.

To fit in better we wore some Indian clothing. Dan went a bit overboard on this. In the movie *Lawrence of Arabia*, there's a scene where Lawrence receives a white robe and turban from his adopted tribe. He accepts the gift and trots off behind a sand dune to try it on. Then he gets weird. He starts pirouetting around like a ballerina. Dan can get equally weird. First he put on traditional Indian pants that could accommodate a water buffalo in each leg. Next he slipped on a flowing pajama overshirt. Then he started fussing with the wraps on his turban to make sure they were just right. Finally satisfied with the look, he started posing. Imagine the Pillsbury Doughboy as a run-way model. I pretty much limited my local clothing to wearing a turban.

My Hat's Off to Turbans

Goal number three on my list was to wear a turban. Prior to the trip, I thought of a turban as a simple piece of traditional clothing, like a tie, but with no real use. I have since learned that it serves many practical purposes.

The turban was first introduced to India by invading tribes. The mushroom-shaped wrapping of cloth around the head may have originally served as a soft helmet to protect the heads of fighters. Over time, local people adopted the turban as traditional headwear. There are many kinds of wrapping patterns for affixing the eight feet or more of cloth to the head. Especially for rural villagers, the turban is more than a fashion statement. We were taught a variety of uses for our turbans.

Depending on your wrap, a flap of cloth can cover the face or back of the neck. In sandstorms, we used the face covering to filter the air we breathed and the weave of the cloth is thin enough that you can see through it like a pair of goggles, keeping the dust out of your eyes. The back flap keeps sun and flies off your neck.

The unwrapped turban is used as a ground cloth to lie on. It also serves as a light blanket to keep away the midnight chill, a use I appreciated many nights. In a pinch, you can use it to filter debris out of drinking water.

A side benefit of wearing a turban is that we were not as noticeable at a distance. We blended in by wearing local clothing, which meant we were less likely to attract crowds.

Crowd Control

As we approached towns, Dan and I fell into a pattern. Dan went into town to reconnoiter a route or shop while I camel-sat. Shopping with camels in tow while you weave through narrow alleys, among food stalls, and under overhanging awnings is not wise. So I became skilled at controlling four camels and the crowd they, or should I say, they and I attracted.

I have a theory about crowds. As a student at the University of California at Berkeley during the Vietnam era when campus demonstrations against the war were common, I remember walking to my Organic Chemistry class and rounding a corner to face a football-stadium sized crowd. Most were innocent campus students like me, but a small group of off-campus demonstrators was taking advantage of the anonymity provided by the crowd. A lone policeman was surrounded by the mob. It must have been terrifying for him. The off-campus demonstrators were pelting him with rocks. I remember thinking, *Wrong. Someone has got to do something.* At that exact moment, a battalion of baton-bashing police rounded the other corner swinging into the students. The crowd surged towards me. I understand why bison run off cliffs. In an adrenalin-inspired stampede I ran a nine-second 100-yard dash and vaulted an eight-foot-high chainlink fence to escape. Several repeat experiences of crowd behavior instilled in me the belief: The bigger the crowd, the bigger the chance of having a jerk who will do something stupid. My theory was proven yet again on this trip.

In one village, Dan split off to shop. Like a relay racer passing a baton, he smoothly handed his camels' reins to me. I tied them to various trees. In minutes, 100 people surrounded our little caravan. The proportion of jerks to crowd size was in effect. As I stood on the ground leaning over a kneeling Raika to adjust her saddle, one man made a clucking sound. In Camelese this means: Stand up as fast as you can. Raika lurched upwards—all 1,400 pounds. I jumped backwards as her wooden saddle shot by my face. It was a close call. The crowd-jerk thought it was very funny. Each time I tried to work over my camels, he would start clucking. I asked him to stop. But he was having too much fun. Others were starting to follow his lead. The group was becoming unruly.

As a second-degree blackbelt, it's been pounded into me to avoid confrontation, turn the other cheek, follow the path of the peaceful warrior. Forget that. I smiled at my heckler and walked towards him. He was standing next to a tree. I stood there relaxed and then casually snapped out a front kick, hitting the tree just above his startled head. Still smiling I pointed at the tree and said, *sir*, the Hindi word for head, and mimicked his clucking sound while pointing at his head. I think he would have made a good charades player because he quickly backed down.

Over time, I tried many crowd-control techniques. I'd politely ask people to leave. They usually ignored me. I tried staring them down, they stared back. I'd ignore them and they would approach closer. I'd tell them, "Dan has contagious leprosy." They would smile and offer to shake hands. Sometimes I reached under one of our packs and then, in a startled voice, yelled *bitu!* (slang for scorpion), and pretended to toss a scorpion into the crowd. This was good for a momentary break. But our fans were hardcore and quickly regrouped around us. My best crowd-scattering move was the camel waltz.

When the crowd got thick and started touching the camels and fondling gear, ignoring my requests to back off, I imagined Yul Brynner in *The King and I* waltzing with Deborah Kerr. With this image in my mind, holding onto all four reins, camel heads lined up, the tune "Shall We Dance" in my head, I pivoted 5,400 pounds of camels around in a waltzing whirl. This was done with the warning, "Watch out, they kick." This invariably gave me breathing space. If I felt really uncomfortable in a crowd, I moved on. Dan knew to continue down the road in the direction where he'd last left me.

Train Station

Four days after leaving Bubbles's fortress, we found ourselves again following a railroad track towards our next destination. The strategy worked well, though there were some concerns. At junctions there were wires running along the ground. These wires controlled the train signals. Occasionally our camels stumbled across these trip wires and I worried that we had just rerouted a train.

That day, dark clouds threatened rain. The rain gods were still following us across the desert. But we were in luck. There was a railway station near the tracks. A wood beam over the doorway was imprinted with the date 1879. It was a classic British-India railway station with a raised veranda, several airy interior rooms, and turban-like turrets. Missing tiles, cracks in the ceiling, graffiti, piles of windblown leaves, and signs of small fires on the floor led us to believe it was abandoned. Two neem trees opposite the back veranda were perfect for tethering the camels as the first drops of rain hit. We set up housekeeping on the veranda. The rain stuck around for two days, as did we. We thought it was better to be sheltered than sitting on moldy saddles.

Later that day, while cooking dinner on the station's steps, a train pulled up. A policeman got off with the rest of the passengers. Apparently, word had traveled that there were two squatters at the abandoned train station. He approached us. What we didn't see were more police sneaking around the building while this man kept our attention. They carried bamboo rods. My guess is that they used the rods to beat tramps who set up camp in train stations. Turns out that it wasn't abandoned after all. I think we would have gotten a thrashing, but at the sight of our skin color, the camels, and our gear, they became very polite. They had heard of the two crazy foreigners riding across India and wished us good luck.

Dan and I spent the rest of the day lounging against our saddles on the station veranda. Covered by our camel blankets and protected from the rain by the station roof, we napped, caught up with writing in our journals, and did an experiment that I have wondered about since I was child. Taking advantage of a break in the rain showers, Dan and I walked over to the railroad tracks. We had figured out the train schedule and expected a train any minute. Carefully, Dan laid an Indian coin, about the size of a quarter, on the track. He then positioned a stick on the railroad ties so that it pointed at the coin. We stepped back and waited. Minutes later the train roared by. After it had passed, Dan used the stick to locate where the coin had been. It was no longer on the track but it lay nearby. It was now the size of a fifty-cent piece. My childhood question had been answered, trains are heavy enough to squash coins.

In between moments of entertainment, there was a logistic problem we faced every day—finding 120 pounds of camel food. Camels eat a lot. Dan was a master at finding local farmers who would sell us camel fodder. There were many evenings when he shouldered empty grain bags and trudged off into the darkness. An hour later he would return lugging full bags himself or enlisting help from local kids or adults. At our train station layover, one of the farmers was especially kind. When we tried to pay, he said in Hindi, "Your God is my God. No payment is necessary." We received many such kindnesses. It was the type of gesture that had a lot to do with our growing affection for India's people.

Every night we had to find enough camel food to fill two large grain bags. Dan and I often fell asleep to the sound of munch-munch-munch.

Rest stops were also an opportunity to set up the computer. I would update our Internet journal and download emails. Emails were sent to us from students in New Zealand, Britain, India, and the U.S. asking questions about our trip. To encourage students to go through our web site, I had drawn cartoons that illustrated various aspects of the trip and answered questions like, What is the longest venomous snake in the world? How long can a camel go without drinking water? Can you really get water from a camel's hump?

Snippets from Our Web Site: www.thecaravanoflight. com

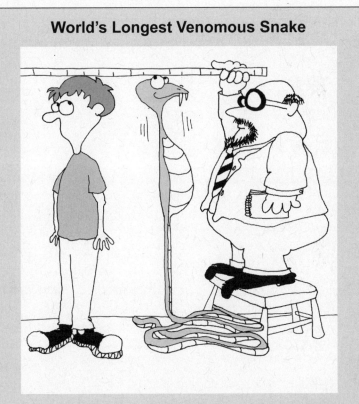

World's Longest Venomous Snake

The king cobra (*Ophiophagus hannah*) is the longest venomous snake in the world. The biggest one ever measured was eighteen and a half feet in length. When threatened, they can rise to the height of a man. Being eye-to-eye with this snake would be pretty scary. Fortunately, king cobras rarely attempt to bite people. In fact they shun human contact. Of the 10,000 deaths every year in India due to snake bite, only a small percentage are caused by king cobras. This snake spends most of its time hunting other snakes.

Anyone Thirsty?

Camels are super-tough animals. They can go without drinking water longer than any other domestic animal. How long they can survive without water depends on a number of factors: their food supply, daytime temperature, nighttime temperature, wind, and whether they are working or resting. In the Sahara, camels go for six to seven months without drinking water. This doesn't mean they don't need water. They get sufficient moisture from the plant material they eat.

As the temperature goes up, camels need to drink more often. At 86° to 95° F (30° to 35° C), camels can go for ten to fifteen days without water. When the temperature reaches 104° F (40° C) and above, camels need more frequent watering. Some breeds of camels can go without water for seven to eight days in the heat of the summer. In Mauritania, where temperatures reach 118° F (48° C) during the day and 86° F (30° C) at night, camels drink every five days, but have gone as long as ten days without water.

A camel can lose up to 40 percent of its weight in water before it is in trouble. A human who loses just 12 percent of his body weight in water is dead. The reason a camel is more resistant to dehydration may be due to the shape of their blood cells. The elliptical, or football-like, shape of a camel's blood cells allow them to pass by one another even when their blood gets thicker with dehydration. A human's rounder blood cells are more likely to get caught in bloodstream traffic jams that plug veins and arteries causing death.

So let's say you and your camel are dehydrated after days in the desert. If you are in a chugging contest with a camel, you will lose. A camel can drink 28 gallons (106 liters) of water at one time. Imagine sitting down and drinking the amount of liquid contained in 56 cartons of milk. Camels have been known to drink 45 gallons (170 liters) in one 24-hour period. That's more than twice the liquid that a standard car gas tank holds. And they drink at a rate of 2.5 to 7 gallons/minute (10 to 27 liters/minute).

People unfamiliar with camels once believed you could get water from a camel's hump. This myth persisted up until 1950. It's thought that the story got started when desperate travelers killed a camel and drank the greenish fluid out of the animal's stomach. This liquid is not exactly water, but as the story got passed down, the place where they got the liquid moved up. Eventually, people who knew little about camels were saying that water was stored in the hump, but this isn't true. The hump is mostly fat. Water is distributed throughout the cells of a camel's body.

The next day we followed the railroad tracks again. They led to the outskirts of Sikar, our first large city after Bikaner. We were now forty-six days into the trip.

Camel Nightmare

Like any other big city, Sikar is surrounded by suburbs. Land speculators use simple brick L's to mark the corners of a plot. Having been raised by real estate-savvy parents, I'm always interested in land prices. These 1,600 square meter plots sell for around 8 *lakhs* ($16,000 USD). At that moment I wanted to buy one so that we would have a place to rest. Soon we hit denser areas of the town. In the distance we saw nonstop buses, trucks, and cars. We decided to back-track in search of a less congested road. The new route took us into a maze of twisting streets and alleys. As the passages narrowed, we came to moats of sewage, forcing us down side alleys. We also attracted a group of thirty to fifty teens. We were more interesting than the cricket match they had been playing. They began to shadow us. Oblivious to the danger of nervous camels and camel owners, they pushed in on us chanting, "What is your name?" "Where are you from?" "How are you?" Answering was futile. They only repeated the phrases again to impress us, and each other, with their command of the English language.

As it got dark, I got frustrated. One teen was particularly annoying. He ignored my repeated warnings in Hindi to back off. He rode his bicycle six inches from Raika who skittered all over the road and into traffic. He began the incessant mantra, "How are you?" "What is your name?" I had an evil thought. I pretended to trip, not hard to do when you are being yanked around by two camels. Stumbling, I aimed my walking stick at his spokes. Direct hit. You'd be surprised how fast a bike stops with a stick jammed in the spokes. I did a good job of looking annoyed at his carelessness in messing up my stick. Other bicycle riders took the hint and backed off. I once heard that all behaviors have an appropriate time and place. Clumsy was in fashion.

We hoped to get through town before nightfall. No such luck. We escaped the maze as the light faded, arriving at the main road through town. We felt a little desperate, like travelers in Transylvania who know it is best to get off the road before sunset. The road was bumper-to-bumper blinding lights, honking horns, and choking exhaust. That's when a gob of shaving cream-like foam splatted on my forehead. My first thought was that my bicycle-spoke friend was getting revenge by squirting shaving cream from an upper window.

I tried to wipe it away with my arm only to find more on my sleeve. In fact, my shirt and turban were covered with the stuff. Looking up I discovered the source.

My camels were foaming at the mouth with fear. Another glob of camel drool plopped onto my shoulder and oozed down the front of my shirt. And here I thought I was just sweaty. This was grossly yucky.

I fought to keep their heads down. A high head, on a stressed camel, indicates camel panic. A lower head gives a handler more control. My hands and arms were burning with the strain of trying to keep their heads down by holding them on a short rein close to their chins. Sometimes they'd lift me off the ground when a bus rumbled by.

Stressed by the dense traffic, Raika and Sam foamed at the mouth. Globs of drool splattered onto my shirt and turban.

Dan and I were resigned to walking all night, if necessary, to escape this traffic nightmare. Periodically, we'd slip into an alley to give the camels and ourselves a break from the traffic. But the curse of the curious crowd followed us. People were oblivious to our repeated requests to stay away from the camels. Our warnings that the camels bite and kick were ignored as people crowded in for a closer look. Two foreigners with camels was too much of a novelty for locals to pass up. So we'd abandon our rest spot and move on to lose the crowd. It was exhausting. At one point, we pulled into the only open space, a gas station. One of the attendants approached us as two of the camels pooped on the clean concrete. He motioned for us to leave.

Here's where our luck changed. The owner of the station came out. We explained our plight. He said, "Feel free to stop as long as you need." Mercifully, he shooed away the beginnings of a crowd.

"We need something to lift our spirits," said Dan. "What would you say if I went back to that ice cream parlor we just passed?"

"Fine. I'll watch the camels."

Dan was gone a long time. When he returned, he handed me an ice cream and said, "I've got two treats. And one is better than ice cream."

"What could be better than ice cream?"

"I met Sachin Maharia. He's the owner of the ice cream shop. I told him about our difficulties. He's invited us to stay at his father's house. It's only a short distance from here." Dan paused, "And get this. They have a separate enclosed courtyard where we can put up the camels."

I would have said no, but when Dan mentioned a place where the camels would be safe, I said, "Let's check it out." Dan knew I wouldn't go for anything where we didn't have camel security in this busy city.

Sachin arrived to lead. The streets leading to his father's house had high walls on either side. Expensive homes were on the other side of those walls.

Sachin told us about himself as we walked, "I have recently completed my business degree."

"Where did you go to school?" I asked.

"A university in France. I have come home with many business ideas. The ice cream shop is a franchise. It is very modern by Indian standards. I require that my employees maintain European standards of cleanliness."

"It's one of the cleanest places I've seen in India," agreed Dan.

"My father owns the 900-seat movie theater next to it. I thought we could increase our profits with the ice cream shop. Customers of the theatre could eat before or after a movie."

"Seems like a good idea," I said, while pushing Raika back so she wouldn't step on my heels.

"It is an upscale shop," said Sachin. "That's why it has a glass front and is not open to the street. In India, a glass front indicates an upscale establishment for an upscale clientele."

When we arrived at the Maharia's home, the first thing Sachin showed us was the enclosed courtyard for the camels. It was perfect. A high-walled enclosure with a metal gate. It even had slabs of concrete for tying up the camels. After securing the camels and removing their loads, we were escorted through a side gate.

It opened onto the back garden of a mansion. The lawn was razor-cut flat, a patio framed it and to the side was a multicar garage. The Maharia's home was lovely. We were introduced to Sachin's father, Randhir Maharia, a successful businessman.

Over the next two days, we were treated royally. A private room and bath were made available to us. Mrs. Maharia cooked an array of delicious Indian dishes. A sightseeing tour of the city was set up. Our clothes were washed. Our camels were fed. And Dan embarrassed me. When he found he could have all the ice cream he could eat at the restaurant for free, he was a bit of a pig. It was hard to blame him though. Everything was ultraclean and the fig-and-honey milkshakes were delicious.

One evening while Dan was sucking up ice cream at the restaurant, I sat on the back terrace with Randhir and discussed some of the problems India faces.

"Electricity may be the undoing of India," explained Mr. Maharia. "You may have noticed all the sprinkler systems in the fields you've passed."

"Yes. Dan and I sometimes ask the farmers if we can stand in the spray to wash our bodies and clothes at the same time."

"Electricity allows the farmers to pump from wells for those sprinklers. This in turn increases crop production. Where cisterns had previously been used to trap rainwater, now it is easier to pump from a well. The cisterns are falling into disuse. Twenty-five years ago the water table was 60 feet down. Due to the use of pumps, the water table has dropped 175 feet down and is now dropping at a rate of 5 feet per year. We are going to run out of water in the future."

"I also noticed that many of these wells are uncovered," I added. "In the U.S., uncapped wells are illegal. It is too easy to contaminate an underground water supply with runoff from sewage or fertilizer." Then I remembered something from my university days when I was trained as a botanist. "There's also a problem with the sprinklers. They are running during the heat of the day. A high percentage of the water evaporates before it has a chance to penetrate to the crop's roots. If the sprinklers were run at night, it could save a lot of water and the water would sink deeper into the soil."

Mr. Maharia nodded.

The next day, Sachin arranged a press conference. We took two camels to the conference for a photo shoot in front of the ice cream parlor. The newspaper photographers wanted us to ride the camels, but we were next to a busy road and resisted their requests. Neither Dan nor I wanted to go galloping down the street chased by a bus and a bunch of reporters. With Sachin serving as interpreter, the journalists asked a variety of questions about our journey. We explained that we had three goals. There was adventure. Then the educational web site that allowed students to follow the adventure. Plus the humanitarian cause of installing a solar-powered lighting system in a remote village. Little did we know that this and future interviews would give us the notoriety to get out of some sticky situations. The following day we appeared in five newspapers and on the local television station.

The rest of the day was spent touring the surrounding area with Sachin as our guide. At one point we drove up a steep road to visit the 1,105-year-old Harshnath Temple. In the distance, as is common in India, we saw the outlines of an ancient fort perched on a sheer-sided mountain. It looked like some fantasy art project. We asked Sachin about it.

"Yes, it is a fort."

"Does anyone live there?" I asked.

"No. No one goes there. It is impossible to get to it."

That word impossible had Dan and I looking at each other. We like tweaking the "im" off of "impossible."

"Have you ever tried to go there?"

"Oh, no. Why would anyone want to go there?"

This blasé attitude towards ancient remnants of their civilization was common in India. If that fort were in America, every kid within miles would have tried to scramble up the sheer walls, just to say he'd done it. But forts are a rupee a dozen in India, and don't seem to hold much attraction, especially if they are hard to reach.

14 राजस्थान पत्रिका

चल साथी चल, तेरे देश को देखें। गांव-गांव जमाेंगे, तुझको सैर कराएंगे- मूक प्राणी ऊंट को साथी बनाकर शायद यही कह रहे हैं ये विदेशी। बीकानेर से काठमाण्डू तक का सफर ऊंट पर तय करने वाले ये दोनों विदेशी मंगलवार को सीकर पहुंचे।

रेगिस्तानी जहाज पर यात्रा का रोमांच

A headline from one of the many Indian news stories covering our journey across India. This photo was taken in front of Sachin's ice cream shop. The headline reads: *The Romance of a Journey on Ships of the Desert.*

On our final day in Sikar, the Maharia family had a ceremony for our departure. We were outfitted in ceremonial turbans. I got a brilliant red turban. I chose red so traffic would see me better. They had also arranged for a camel man from a local village to help guide us through Sikar. Sachin led the way on his motorcycle. When the traffic became problematic, Sachin wheeled his cycle across the road like a highway patrol officer and blocked traffic until we passed. The press coverage guaranteed that everyone knew who we were. Well-wishers shouted greetings and encouragement along the route. With Sam and Raika pressed against my shoulders we powered down the street in our own mini-parade. Soon we were out of town and on our way.

An octopus is better equipped for riding a camel. You need two hands to hold the reins, one rein in each hand. A third hand would be helpful to clutch a rope lashed across the saddle. We call this lashing the "sissy bar." Holding the sissy bar may save you from going airborne when your camel goes bronco. A fourth hand is necessary to hold the reins of the camel you are towing. This whole arrangement falls apart when your riding camel is in a foul mood. Without warning she will spin. This is why you hold the towline of your pack camel in your hand. If the line were tied off, you would get tangled in the rope. Entanglement causes the line to viciously yank on the tow camel's nose pegs. Now you have two enraged side-by-side camels with you wrapped in the middle. Holding a towline allows you to whip it over your head, taking care not to strangle yourself in the process. An alternative is to cast off the towline and deal with your riding camel first. Raika, in particular, liked to test my reactions.

Later that day, we accepted a farmer's hospitality to camp out in his field. He provided us with rope beds, feed for our camels, hot tea, and tractor music. We thought the obnoxiously loud religious chants that lasted all night were bad. Tractors are worse. Farmers contract with tractor owners to plow their fields. Because of the expense of a tractor, and because tractor owners wanted to quickly earn back their investment, they operate on a twenty-four-hour schedule. The tractor only stops if it breaks down or needs to be refueled. The only way you can sleep while a tractor circles your campsite is if you are deaf or have a concussion. As the morning sun rose, two bleary-eyed cameleers brooded over the neat furrows that snaked around our bedding and gear.

As we departed tractor central the next morning, an elderly man from the farm asked for a ride to the train station. Dan obliged by having GB kneel down. GB was the least likely to try and throw our passenger. This old man had known camels as a youth, but hadn't ridden in years. He grinned like a ten-year-old in a candy shop and talked to everyone we passed.

This far from the desert, camels were no longer a common sight. They thinned out as the farms got bigger. Large farms make it economically feasible to replace camels with tractor muscle. A senator's assistant in Sikar told us, "I admire your courage. I'm Indian, yet I feel uncomfortable around camels. Indians are getting further from the animals and the land we once knew so well."

Back on the main road, we came across a truck weigh-in station. Commercial trucks using the highway had to pay a fee. The fee depended on their weight. The top of the scale was a large steel plate set flush to the ground and big enough to handle the largest truck. Walking up to the scales, I held out some money to the surprised attendant. "Please weigh us," I said. It only took a moment to maneuver our camels onto the platform. Four camels, all our gear, an old man, Dan, and I weighed in at 5,800 pounds.

This was also a chance to check our progress. We were averaging six and a half miles a day. A great day had been twelve miles, far short of the distances we had calculated when planning the trip. We were now at day fifty of the trip. The logistics of finding camel food, human food, water, and campsites, along with the occasional rainstorm and difficulties packing the camels, put a crimp in our plans. Even though we were slow, we were proud of our route-finding accuracy.

Camel Switch

Considering that we relied on a simple road map, rather than the high-tech equipment we had originally brought for the trip, we did a great job at staying on course. Our method was simple. We looked at the road map to locate a village along our route. Then we asked directions to this village from everyone we passed. Often one person pointed one way, then the next person pointed in the opposite direction. We made our choice a democratic process. We let as many people as possible vote on the direction. By asking the same question enough times, the majority pointed us in the right direction.

My favorite route-finding technique was the riverboat captain method. Only there was no riverboat and no water. We navigated dry riverbeds. Several waterless channels showed on our map. If a riverbed meandered in the direction we were headed, we clambered down the embankment and followed the sandy course. This was also the part of the trip where I decided to try a new riding camel. You might say I switched camels in mid-dry river.

"Dan, I've had it with Raika," I said, in irritation. "I almost wish I'd taken Katea-ram's advice and put a needle in her nose peg."

"Having a bit of a problem?" asked Dan as he stroked GB's neck.

"Problem," I fumed. "She still freaks out when a bicycle goes by. That iron nose of hers makes it impossible to control her in traffic. I can pull on her reins hard enough to break them, and she ignores me. I've lost track of how many times I've had to jump off at a full gallop just to keep her from killing both of us. Plus, she makes Sam and Humper miserable. I swear she gets pleasure in tangling their reins and ripping off their nose pegs."

"Maybe you need some pointers from the camel master," replied Dan. "GB and I are getting along famously."

I gritted my teeth, "Enough with the camel whisperer. GB is not Raika. GB pulled carts around traffic before we got her. She's older and more mature. Raika is a schizophrenic dingbat."

"A bit testy are we?" asked Dan.

Nearby, Raika was threatening to bite Sam's neck.

"Look, she's going mental again." I yelled in Raika's direction hoping to distract her. She looked at me like I was a camel's version of a dork and went back to threatening Sam.

"That does it," I said, pulling a riding saddle off the ground. "I'm riding Sam. Let's stick to the riverbed for a while. If she throws me, at least I will land on soft sand."

After only an hour of practice, Sam responded better than Raika.

An hour later I rode up next to Dan, "Sam feels safer than Raika. You probably don't remember, but originally I wanted Sam to be my riding camel."

"I remember," said Dan. "But the camel men said that Raika would make the better riding camel."

"So much for the experts," I replied sarcastically. I should have gone with my gut instinct. When Sam's owner showed her to me, he reached into her mouth and grabbed her tongue. I figured any camel that allowed its tongue to be grabbed had to be pretty mellow.

Raika was stripped of her riding saddle and demoted to pack camel. Sam became my new riding camel.

The change in Sam over the next few days was remarkable. It was as if she'd received a booster shot of self-esteem. Not being behind Raika as the pack camel, she didn't have to worry about getting kicked, stepping in Raika's poop, or having her peg lines yanked. She seemed grateful for her new position and nuzzled me. Raika on the other hand was totally miffed at the new situation. She bit at me when I tried to load bags on her saddle. She rolled in the sand to get rid of her pack. She even tried cutting Sam off to get back in front. Raika may have been a camel but she displayed the traits of a jealous and spiteful human.

This didn't mean Sam was ideal. Unfortunately, I'd invested weeks of riding training in Raika. Sam was being asked to step up with virtually no practice. But even when we had problems, it was as if Sam was trying to understand what I wanted, while Raika had the attitude of a snotty prom queen.

I swore that Raika took pleasure in Sam's shortcomings. For example, Raika was a big-boned heavily muscled camel. When she kneeled, she stretched out one leg slowly, then lowered herself to her other knee as if she was curtsying to the queen. Her rising was equally regal. She looked as if she was posing for a camel fashion magazine. After gracefully rising or lowering, Raika looked over at Sam disdainfully. Sam wasn't graceful. To lower herself, Sam folded up both knees like a cheap lawn chair and crashed to the ground. Getting up was even worse. She stuck a rear leg way out to the side as if she was going to do the splits. Then she rocked back and forth to get enough momentum to bring her other leg up. Often it looked like she wouldn't make it. It was embarrassing. Villagers would actually laugh and point at Sam's ungainly yoga poses. I felt sorry for her and avoided having villagers around when she rose or knelt. She had the grace of a three-legged water buffalo, but Sam made me feel safer than Raika.

Camel Talk V

At the water trough, GB slipped up next to Sam.

"Keep a tight tail," said GB in a whisper.

"What?"

"Raika is not happy with the food giver putting the riding saddle on you. She says she will bite your tail off if she must follow you."

"I don't care. It is better than having her tangle my nose lines and ripping out my pegs. My nose feels like I've run into a thorn tree. I can taste the pus. If I have my pegs broken one more time because of her I will bite *her* tail off."

"Maybe you are learning," said GB nodding.

"So are the food givers. They don't tie Humper or me next to Raika at night."

"They are learning," said GB. "Did you see what the thin food giver did when Raika rolled in the sand to get rid of her carrying load?"

"No," said Sam.

"Just before it happened," said GB, "Raika told me she was going to teach the food giver a lesson. She would not be treated like a lowly pack camel. She would crush her load. Instead, she was taught a lesson. When she started rolling on the ground, the thin food giver didn't try to make her rise. He did the opposite. He threw all his weight on her hump and held her to the sand. You should have seen her struggle and kick. Her eyes turned white with fear."

Sam understood. For a camel to lie down of its own choice was one thing. To be trapped in that position was terrifying.

"She won't be so ready to roll again," said GB. "The food givers are learning. I'm even beginning to like my food giver."

"Really!"

"He doesn't beat me or make me pull a heavy cart like my last food giver."

Jungle Temple

Not long after changing camels, the terrain changed. We found ourselves in hilly country with dense scrub and thorn trees. The trees had two-inch long spikes that tore at our pants, shirts, and hats. It was a jungle with teeth. Spots of blood appeared on our clothing. I used my gloved hands to fend off the wicked branches. The camels didn't mind rubbing up against a tree that could shred human flesh. Their hides were so thick, they treated the trees like a back scratcher—good way to get rid of an itch. The problem was that Dan and I were the "itch." This meant Dan and I had to bob, weave, and slide to the side of our saddles to avoid being scraped off. Dan, who was leading, would occasionally have his hat plucked off by a spiny overhead branch. The trail was too narrow to turn around, so I'd retrieve his hat while trying to keep my own hat on my head. I thought, *Next time I'm bringing a suit of armor.*

Eventually we came to a main road. Off to the side we saw a moss-covered dome and minarets poking above the trees. We detoured down a path leading towards the ruins. The locals called this place Nagagee. Monkeys frolicked in a many-rooted banyan tree in front of an abandoned temple. We dismounted to explore. Steep stairs led up to chambers, their ceilings covered with eroding scenes of elephants and Indian deities. Roots lifted the paving stones. Other plants growing on the roof snaked their roots down into the chambers and laced the walls. Broken statuary littered the temple grounds. Some of the statues looked ancient. Their only protection from souvenir hunters is that they are cursed. It is said that anyone who removes them will be plagued by bad luck.

This classic adventure scene of an abandoned temple in the jungle was spoiled somewhat by a *sadhu* (holy man) seated cross-legged near the ruin. He had long black straggly hair, a red dot in the middle of his forehead, and a simple wrap of cloth around his waist. What didn't fit was the loud radio blaring next to him. It sounded like he was listening to a soccer match with frequent commercial breaks that included the familiar words, "Coca Cola."

Portions of the ruined temple at Nagagee. Only monkeys live there now.

We continued farther up the path and were greeted by another sadhu. He invited us back to the new monastery that replaced the original temple. The modern structure was a boxy concrete building. There was none of the charm of the abandoned temple. Here we were introduced to the head priest. We were told he was one hundred years old. He looked more like fifty. We were also informed that he hadn't left the monastery for the past fifty years.

If this is true, all those people who have been cryogenically frozen in the hopes of being brought back to life in the future should have come to live here. It looked like it would add a hundred years to your life span. The sadhu blessed me and put a spot of red dye on my forehead. Politeness required that I accept this forehead graffiti. The problem occurs when you start sweating. The red dye dribbles off your forehead and stains your clothes. Dan, who sweats a lot, already looked like he had a nose bleed.

A *sadhu*, holy man, greeted us at the entrance to the new temple at Nagagee. We were told that he was one hundred years old but he looked like he wasn't a day over fifty.

The next couple of days found us riding along dry riverbeds, through grass above our camels' heads, and down narrow country lanes. One evening we set up camp in the sand of a waterless riverbed. There was an ancient fort on the ridge to our right. A hill to our left was capped by a temple that glowed eggshell blue in the soft light. A quarter-moon was visible. Our camels munched neem leaves, in time to a chant from a nearby monastery. We watched several monks walking along the riverbed looking for a suitable place to poop.

Pooping

In the Western world, pooping is a razzle-dazzle science. Billion-dollar industries are supported by poop. Porcelain thrones, water pumps, breather pipes, buried pipes, flush valves, filler valves, siphons, sewage treatment plants, and Tidy Bowl rinse—it takes a college degree in toiletology to understand how it all works. In rural India, things are simple.

Without toilets, people defecate in the fields, along the road, and at the entrance to and exit from villages. Turds rule. This wouldn't be so bad, except for one thing. In America, every back-packing Boy Scout and Girl Scout has been taught to copy a cat. Bury it. Not so in India. There are no ca-ca funerals with full burial. It sits on the ground in plain sight. You can smell a village coming and going. This oversight was a great mystery until one morning. Scurrying barefoot out to a field for a sunrise sit-down, I tried kicking a cat hole in the soil. It was not practical in bare feet. Barefoot or sandal-wearing villagers would have the same excavation problems. A lack of shoes leads to different hygiene standards.

Many of the hygienic standards taken for granted in the U.S. don't apply in India. Adventurers have to deal with local customs and find ways to stay healthy. In particular I wasn't keen on shaking hands. That's because people use their hands in place of toilet paper. Supposedly, only the left hand is used to wipe. That's why it is considered extremely impolite to eat or serve someone with your left hand. Maybe it is also the reason that most Indians greet each other by putting both hands together in a praying motion and bow-ing. That way you don't have to touch hands. Unfortunately, when Indians meet foreigners, they think they have to shake hands.

When I became self-righteous about our superior use of toilet paper, Dan offered another viewpoint, "Some of the people say we stink. They say, 'You just use a piece of paper. We at least wash our hands and bottoms afterwards.'" Usually a can of water is carried for this purpose, though we saw people using sand or dust as well.

When I said we saw this, it is because privacy was also at a different level. Sometimes privacy was denied in the most intimate settings. To have people follow you into a field when you are on the verge of diarrhea stretches the patience of the most experienced traveler. In one instance a man followed me and kept asking, "What is your name?" I waved him off, but he continued to pursue me. Realizing there was no escape and close to an "accident," I dropped my drawers and squatted. He insistently repeated, "What is your name?" I politely replied, "I'mapoophead." Walking back to the camels, when other locals would ask, "What is your name?" I pointed to my pursuer who delightedly repeated, "I'mapoophead."

On the topic of waste, Dan and I failed as eco-warriors. Travel books point out that you should, "Take only pictures and leave no waste." Easier written than practiced. Our decline started with water. Guidebooks primly advise against bottled water due to all the plastic bottles that are left behind. The books recommend that you purify your own water. We tried, but found that iodine tablets reacted with the high salt content of desert well water to create a brown scum, a real turn-off for Western water wimps. Plus, as a past water chemist, I worried that the iodine's bacteria-killing power was compromised by its reaction with the salt. Our ultra-modern Miox purifiers posed another problem. These purifiers use salt, water, and an electric charge to produce a chlorine disinfectant. Advertised to clean anything from a mountain stream to septic tank waste, we found it necessary to add a chlorine dose higher than found in a swimming pool to get the test strips to register, "Safe." Warm, salty, heavily chlorinated water? Nope. So we ended up buying gallons of water in plastic bottles. This wasn't all bad. Local villagers don't have ready access to storage containers. We'd hand our empties to village kids who seemed delighted with our recycling.

Food waste wasn't a problem. Anything edible left out was immediately scavenged by goats, pigs, sheep, cows, ants, or humans. Even the local plates, made from woven leaves, were gobbled by the animals. The real problems were aluminum foil, plastic wrappers, and empty cans. One time when we handed our waste to a shop-keeper to dispose of, he casually threw it into the street. Some of the poorest people go through this refuse to find anything that may be remotely salvageable. Only the really useless junk gets left behind.

Dan's Bear

Good Mom, bad son. That is how we defined our next encounter. A farmer had granted us permission to stay in his field for the evening. When we inquired about buying camel feed, his son got into the act. Sure, he'd sell us feed. He brought Dan to his home. Dan was offered fodder that didn't look like anything our camels had eaten before. The son assured us it was first rate. Dan loaded up eighty pounds to bring back. That's when the son's mother stepped in. She refused to let Dan pay for the feed. The son grew angry. Sharp words were exchanged. He pushed her and called her a stupid old woman. She stood her ground. Dan was embarrassed for her. In India, such rude behavior from a son is uncommon. But Mom was insistent, "Don't pay." When Dan got back, our hungry camels got antsy when they saw the stuffed feedbags. They were hungry. When the contents were poured out, they looked disappointed. They wouldn't touch it. Later we found out that the son was trying to rip off two inexperienced foreigners. The "feed" was chaff used to stuff cushions. It had as much food value as styrofoam. Not even a starving animal would eat it. Mom had prevented her clever son from cheating us.

That evening some of the son's intoxicated friends drifted into the field where we were staying. They were in good spirits and a little raucous. Part of this was Dan's fault. He carried one item that made it hard to get rid of crowds. Every night, Big British Adventurer Dan Wright fell asleep with a teddy bear cuddled in his arms.

Villagers were fascinated by his ragged little bear. They stared, pointed, and laughed. I tried to get Dan to ditch the bear. His reply, "You junk your camera equipment, I'll junk the bear." Our present audience was either making fun of the bear or the foreigner who slept with a stuffed animal. That is when they offered us cigarettes and alcohol. Dan, his bear, and I politely declined. Then a water pipe arrived with opium. They insisted we try it. We were equally insistent and repeated Nancy Reagan's formula of "Just say no." Things were getting uncomfortable.

My inner voice said, "Get them out of here now, before they get any more stoned." I took advantage of being 6' 4" and moved in on them repeating *Subhratri* (good night). They didn't want to leave. I kept repeating the phrase and pushing into their space. Reluctantly they moved off a short distance. I could hear the word *gora* (an insulting word for foreigner) interspersed with laughter. I found myself waking up periodically during the night to make sure our drugged visitors didn't return. It made for a fitful sleep.

The next day we were glad to leave.

Dan and his crowd-attracting bear. Dan is
the one on the right.

Dan lounges on a rope bed provided by a farmer while the locals watch his every move. His bear guaranteed they would stand there until dark.

Estimating Distance

While Dan and I were great at staying on course, we had trouble estimating distances. If we saw a range of hills ahead of us, we often guessed aloud how long it would take to get there. We were usually wrong.

"Dan, what do you think that is up ahead?" I asked, pointing into the distance.

"Beggar it if I know," said Dan.

We squinted at a faraway hill. It sparkled back at us.

"It looks like a hill of mirrors," I said.

"Fancy we take a look?"

"Absolutely," I replied. "How long do you think it will take to get there?"

"Maybe a half-hour."

"Normally I would agree. But I've been rotten at judging distance on this trip. My estimates are always high."

Thinking about it, Dan said, "Me too."

"It's probably because we are mountain guides."

"What does that have to do with it?"

"Both of us are accustomed to judging how far away something is by paying attention to the amount of detail we see on a familiar distant object. The further away the object, the more indistinct it becomes. Something that is really far away not only becomes hazy but takes on a bluish tint as well. In the Sierra where I guide, and in Nepal where you lead trips, the air is crystal clear. The air here is polluted by cooking fires, dust from the fields, and smog. Things don't have to be as far away to lose their detail and take on that blue cast. I'm guessing that hill is less than thirty minutes away. I bet we get there in twenty minutes."

I was right. Twenty minutes later we stood at the foot of the knoll. It was composed of dark volcanic rock, a blister on an otherwise flat landscape. Closer inspection explained the sparkle we had seen in the distance. Chunks of glistening mica were embedded in the stone. It was if someone had loaded a cannon with diamonds and blasted the hill. On the north side, a steep rock stairway led up to the ruins of a monastery.

Centuries ago, some holy man had discovered this mysterious geological formation. Certain that it was a sign from the gods, he convinced a religious archi-

Glistening chunks of mica gave this mound of rock a strange appearance. The ruins of a monastery were reached by climbing steep stairs.

tect to build the walls we now stood on. It was a spiritual moment for us. Some of our concerns were not so spiritual.

Bathing in Camel Troughs

It had been several weeks since we had left the mansion in Sikar. Riding, sleeping, and sweating in our clothes had turned us into The Kings of Stink. Dan's boots gave off a stench that would repel skunks. It is said that the worst smell in the world comes from the Corpse Flower, an odor described as a mixture of rotting fish, a decaying elephant corpse, and burnt sugar. We smelled worse. Even our camels puckered their noses when we got upwind. It was at times like these that Dan's lack of shyness made him a legend in my eyes. Dan was on the lookout for the most expensive home he could find.

Eventually we came across a high fenced, wrought iron gated, minicountry mansion. Dan winked at me as he handed off the reins to his camels. I was left watching the camels at the gate, looking woebegone, while Dan approached the house calling out the greeting *Namaste*. When the surprised homeowner met him at the door, Dan politely asked "Can we wash some clothing at your well?" The gates of hospitality swung open. Hallelujah! A servant prepared lunch while we sat on the verandah and discussed the finer points of camels with the family. Then a four-inch irrigation pipe was unhooked from the fields. "Would you like to bathe? Give us your clothes and we will wash them." Dan and I stripped and swam in one of the troughs under the thundering irrigation pump. The dirt was blasted out of our pores. Clean and refreshed, we were now prepared to ride through a tiger reserve.

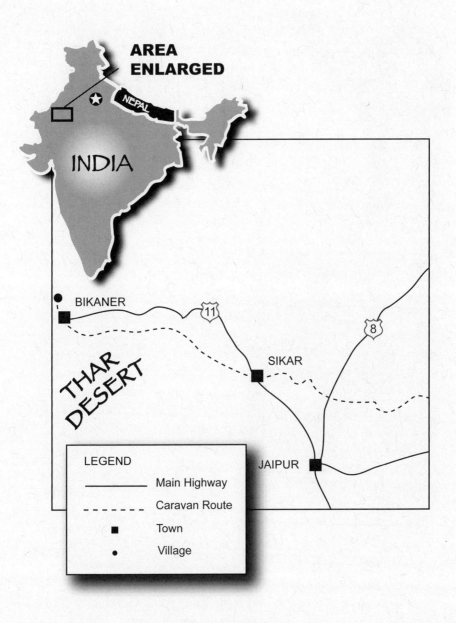

8 Walking Through a Tiger Reserve

A monkey mom and her baby at the Sariska Tiger Reserve

At the outskirts to the Sariska Tiger Reserve, we were greeted by *Planet of the Apes*. Hordes of monkeys lounged along the sides of the road: mothers with babies clinging to their chests, male monkeys watching passing cars with a bored look, and juveniles tumbling about in mock battles. When a passing car tossed out a clump of bananas, there was a flurry of simian grabbing, leaping, scampering, and banana mouth-stuffing. A bush-munching nilgai watched over the monkey antics. A big mongoose skittered into the undergrowth.

Compared to the heavily human populated areas we had traveled through, the wild animals and vegetation were dense in the Sariska reserve. We looked for something official, maybe a fence, to indicate we were in the park. There was no fence, just a sign indicating we were now in the park. Later, local villagers told us, "Tigers have been seen where you are riding. You have just as good a chance of meeting a tiger on the road, maybe even better, as in the jungle."

Signs indicated that big trucks were banned from the road. This was because several tigers had been struck and killed by vehicles. Tigers, just like deer, can be stunned and frozen by the headlights of an approaching vehicle. The prohibition against trucks was to prevent tiger road kill. Of course the ban had not stopped truck traffic. The short cut through the Sariska reserve was just too good for truckers to take the long gas-guzzling detour around the park.

I asked a park ranger, "Have there been any tiger attacks on humans?"

The response was surprising. "No tiger attacks."

Having learned that it is a good idea to ask a question several times in a variety of ways to get at the answer, I asked, "No attacks? So a tiger has never killed a human in the park?"

"There have been no attacks," said the ranger, "But there have been tiger accidents."

"Accidents?"

"Yes. In one case a man went down an embankment to relieve himself under a bridge. A tiger hiding under the bridge killed the man. In another case, a tiger killed a girl who was defending her livestock."

A lawyer would appreciate the fact that the intent of the tiger was taken into account. The tigers were not hunting humans. The tigers simply got caught in a series of unfortunate events. As long as the tiger did not eat the human it had killed, it was a case of unintentional manslaughter, not murder. Locals assured us there was no cause for concern. It was not very reassuring advice for two camel-riding foreigners.

There were three places to stay in Sariska. One was the Pink Palace, a converted maharajah's hunting lodge, at a ridiculous $120 U.S. a night. The second choice was a midrange government-run hotel, the Tiger Den, at $14 a night. The last option was a guest house on the reserve that required special permission.

The guard at the Pink Palace blocked us from passing through the pink gates. When he saw the camels, he said disdainfully, "Camel riders are not welcome in an upper-scale establishment." We tried reasoning with him but he refused to budge.

Then I said, "Tell you what. My friend will hold the camels outside the gate. I'm interested in seeing if we would even want to stay here."

"You must pay 500 rupees ($10 U.S.) to enter the grounds."

"Five hundred rupees just to look? You've got to be joking." He wasn't. Dan and I turned away in disgust.

The Tiger Den staff were also adamant. Anyone with camels as part of their luggage would be turned away.

Our final option, the guest house, was already booked. We knew what Mary and Joseph felt like when they were turned away from the inn.

We visited the Sariska park office where a flustered administrator didn't know what to do with us. We asked for permission to camp in the park. At first it was no, then yes, then no. Finally he said, "Yes." This started our ride on the red tape yo-yo. We were escorted to an open grass field. We tethered the camels and set up our tents.

A short time later a groundskeeper arrived, "It is against regulations to camp in the park. You will be arrested if you don't leave."

"We just got permission to camp from one of the park administrators."

He shook his head, "You must leave."

It was starting to get dark, and the idea of leading our camels along the road in the dark with tigers prowling about did not appeal to us.

While Dan went to find an official, the Field Director of the park, Priyaranjan, another administrator, summoned me. I explained the predicament of having to pack camels in the dark and head down the road in an area we weren't familiar with. He said we could stay. This stay-go-stay-go situation continued for several days. In the morning they would tell us to pack up, by afternoon they would say we could stay, then in the evening they wanted us out of the park again. They didn't know what to do with us. A point in our favor was a British Broadcasting Corporation (BBC) interview. Using our satellite phone, Dan had a weekly live interview with a radio station in England. We explained to park officials that we would cancel the program on the park if we were forced to leave. This threw a bolt into the bureaucratic machinery. Regulations said go, free publicity said stay.

We received special permission to camp. Our tents were pitched close to the camels. I'm not sure if it was because we were protecting the camels or we felt the camels might protect us. As the moon rose, high-pitched barks were followed by the silhouettes of jackals running past our tents.

The following morning, I was lounging at camp, while Dan was off squabbling with officials over our status as park squatters. That's when an official jeep, flashing a blue light, pulled up next to my tent. I thought, *Oh, oh. Looks like the sheriff has come to roust the riff-raff.* The gentleman introduced himself, "My name is Ashutosh A. Teli, an assistant to the Subdivisional Magistrate managing the Alwar District." He didn't seem the least bit antagonistic and asked what I was up to. I gave the standard educational-humanitarian-adventure sound bite. I was more than a little confused about his purpose. Was he going to ask us to leave or not? Apparently he was equally confused. He had just been driving by when he had seen our camels in the field. Curiosity tweaked, he had come over to investigate. He asked what we needed, and I explained we were trying to get into the Tiger Den Hotel and needed a place to put up our camels. He sent one of his assistants to talk to the hotel personnel.

It's not clear if Dan's insistence or Ashutosh's assistant got some action going in our favor, but we got into the hotel. The camels would stay in a nearby field. We exchanged numbers and Ashutosh said he'd be in touch. "I know of villages that would benefit from the solar lighting system you are carrying. We will talk later."

Stomach Demons

That evening we entered the hotel and a demon entered my stomach. Getting sick on an adventure is miserable. We tried preventing illness by drinking purified water, eating foods we peeled ourselves (bananas, oranges, eggs), cleaning vegetables like tomatoes in a chlorine solution, washing hands before meals, and brushing our teeth with purified water. Sometimes even with all the precautions, the tummy critters slipped past our defenses. There were lots of opportunities. They might sneak in when our camels dribbled water over our heads after drinking, or we forgot to wash our hands before handling a mint or Lifesaver. Eating at a roadside café held risks. Even peeling an onion, our hands could pick up bacteria on the outside skin and contaminate the inner portion.

That night I staggered into the bathroom fifteen times. I was the Ex-lax poster boy. My biggest concern was becoming seriously dehydrated. Dan played nurse. He made me swallow a black currant electrolyte replacement drink from our first aid supplies. It was vile stuff. I didn't want to eat or drink. All I wanted to do was sleep. But sleep was difficult. Monkeys bounced and screeched on our balcony. They were obnoxious neighbors. Occasionally they'd test the screen door to see if we had latched it. The rattling door was like an alarm going off, and I would wake up. They were notorious for coming into rooms in search of food.

The next morning park officials changed their minds again. They informed us we'd have to move the camels out of the park. This new directive occurred after Dan had completed his BBC interview inside the park. We could no longer use the interview as a lever to get what we wanted.

Dan arranged for an appointment with the director. After waiting over an hour for the meeting, with no explanation for the delay, Dan decided to get their attention. There was that lack of shyness again. Walking up and down the corridor, he whistled a loud tune. Soon people were coming out of their offices asking him to be quiet. Dan continued until someone asked what he wanted. Dan explained the rudeness with which he had been kept waiting and their new directive to move the camels. No apology was given. He was told to move the camels or else. Normally we would have simply ridden off into the sunset, but I was sick. It made more sense to ride the illness out at the hotel. Dan, resourceful as ever, got recommendations from the park rangers and found a farmer several miles from the park who agreed to watch the camels while I recovered at the hotel.

Vipers

While I languished in bed, Dan visited nearby towns like Thana Gazi and Alwar. He also toured the reserve looking for tigers. You'd think looking for tigers in an open-air jeep would be the most hazardous activity in the park. It wasn't. Dan's most dangerous encounter occurred at the hotel.

While going down a flight of stairs in the dark, Dan stepped on something soft. Pointing his flashlight down at his foot, he saw the head of a viper sticking out from under his sandal. Dan sprang back out of striking range. Fortunately, he had stepped on this poisonous snake just behind the head so that it wasn't able to bite him. If he had stepped on the tail it would have certainly sunk its venomous fangs into his unprotected foot. When he reported the snake to the hotel staff, they said, "Sir, I can assure you there are no snakes out at night. The temperatures are too low for them. I'm sure you are mistaken." In other words, it was a foreigner's imagination playing tricks. Dan was quite miffed. "They treated me like a twit who doesn't know the difference between a snake and a rope," he fumed.

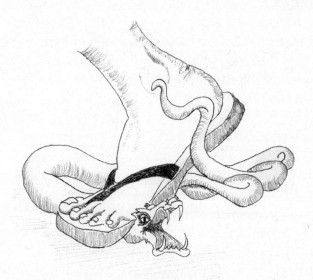

Dan had a close call with a poisonous pit viper. If he had stepped on the snake closer to the tail it would have bitten his sandaled foot.

Several evenings later I was following Dan as he stepped over a low stone wall at the hotel. Suddenly he stopped. Lying on the step on the other side of the wall was a viper. While I kept an eye on the snake, Dan went to roust the hotel employees. "Yes, it is definitely a poisonous snake," they said. We asked them to note that the "snake was out in late night temperatures." As the snake slithered into the undergrowth, Dan tried to hook it with a stick and toss it into an open area. I wasn't sure, but I thought he was trying to fling the snake rather close to the hotel employees. The frightened staff backed far away. I encouraged Dan's snake wrangling as I snapped pictures. We wanted proof that the snake existed for any other hotel staff who might say, "Sir, I'm sure you are mistaken."

Let There Be Light

After four days of rest I felt weak but better. That's when we got a call from Ashutosh, the assistant magistrate who had earlier shown a keen interest in our expedition. "I think I have found a village where you can install the solar-lighting system we talked about," said Ashutosh.

"The village, Dwar Mala, is on a high ridge overlooking the valley," said Ashutosh. "It has no electricity or plumbing. It's quite isolated. Recently, we had some children come down for an educational assessment. It was the first time they saw roads, cars, and shops. Can I send a jeep to pick you up at 6:30 this evening?"

Like an idiot, I said, "Yes." Even as weak as a worm, I didn't want to miss this opportunity.

The jeep arrived, and after a side trip to get Ashutosh, we drove out into the country. At 9:00 P.M. we arrived at the foot of an escarpment, the beginning of a steep hike up to the village. Still not quite recovered from my bout with tummy tigers, I wondered whether I'd be able to make it to the top. But there was no way I was going to miss this. I started up the two-mile trail. I've climbed peaks over 20,000 feet high. What I faced here was a mere hill compared to those mountains, but this climb ranks among my most challenging.

"You all right?" asked Dan.

"Breathing is like trying to suck a bowling ball through a garden hose," I gasped. "When's the next rest stop?"

"Let me take your backpack," offered one of Ashutosh's assistants.

I handed it over gratefully and accepted a walking staff in return.

"Man, this must be what it feels like to be old," I wheezed.

I was oblivious to the moonlit landscape as we ascended the steep trail above the valley. Not having eaten for four days, and being bed-ridden and dehydrated, were taking their toll. All I wanted to do was curl up on the stony trail and take a nap.

We arrived in Dwar Mala late that evening. There were eighty mud-plastered huts with thatched roofs spread across the ridge. Five hundred ninety-one people lived here. Walking around a number of shoulder-high rock walls, we arrived at a yard in front of the headman's house. The glow of a kerosene lamp lit up the faces of turbaned men. They had heard we were coming and were waiting for us. Some men smoked a hookah water pipe. We were escorted to a raised patio. This platform, the size of four picnic tables, had two woven beds for guests. I thankfully collapsed on one of the beds. As is the custom, we were offered tea.

The mud-walled and thatched roof hut we would stay in was open on two sides, with a wonderful breeze blowing through. Water buffalo lounged around the homes. The village relies on water buffalos for milk. This rich milk is used as food and the extra is sold to make money for purchasing other items.

Dwar Mala is one of many villages on a ridgetop that extends for miles. During the rainy season, water is collected in shallow ponds for animals and personal use. In the summer, or during a drought, drinking water is carried up the steep trail we had just climbed.

Energized by our arrival and an audience, I pulled out our solar LED system and set it up so the villagers could see how much illumination it provided. The village elders nodded their heads as Ashutosh explained the system in Hindi. Then came another of the many coincidences we experienced on the trip. The next day, in a village that had never seen foreigners before, a delegation from the Aga Khan Foundation in Delhi and the Bodh Foundation from Rajasthan would arrive to dedicate the installation of a new teacher and a program to encourage the education of girls. This program included a homework section, which needed nighttime lighting. The very thing we were going to install.

As I dropped off to sleep, the village met to decide on the best location for our light installation. The next morning we were shown to a hut that children of the village could use for evening study. As Dan and I thought about the installation we realized the solar panel would have to be mounted on the roof. If it was at ground level, the free-ranging water buffalo could damage it. The angle of the roof required a major engineering effort.

The village elders of Dwar Mala smoked a waterpipe as they discussed the best location for the solar panel we were going to install.

"Dan, we need a frame to hold the solar panel," I said. "The roof doesn't have the right angle to catch the maximum amount of sunlight."

"What do you have in mind?" asked Dan.

I showed him a quick sketch. "Can you build a model out of twigs? Then use the model to explain to the villagers what we are trying to do and that we need their help."

The villagers watched in amusement as Dan went about building a model. They had no idea what he was doing. When he showed it to them, they looked doubtfully at the much larger solar panel it was to support. They were obviously confused. "I think the problem is that they think the model is the final product," I said. "They need to understand that this is only a model."

Using his hands, Dan mimed that he needed their help to make a bigger frame.

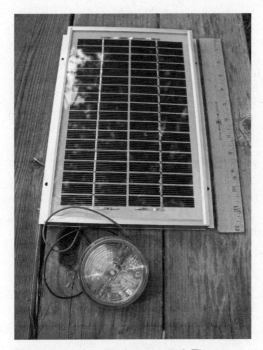

This is the solar panel we carried. The one-foot ruler gives an idea of the size. At the bottom of the picture is a light emitting diode (LED) lamp. The battery, not shown, is the size of tissue box. The solar panel charges the battery during daylight hours. The LED lamps have a life span of 100,000 hours. The solar panels can last 20+ years.

Eventually the villagers assembled the tools we needed, an axe, a saw, and a rope-driven drill. While Dan oversaw the building of the solar frame out of tree branches, I did the electrical wiring inside the hut. Then Dan climbed on top of the roof. I watched from inside as the roof bulged inwards under his weight. I expected to see him crash through the roof any minute. But he must have lost some weight during the trip just as I had. He mounted the framework without a hitch and fed the wires from the solar panel through the roofing straw. I connected the wires to the battery and LEDs. When we were finally ready to test the system there wasn't a villager to be seen. Earlier, they had begged us to take a break from the installation because they wanted us to be part of a big party that was originally arranged for the arriving delegation from Delhi. There was going to be food, and speeches, introductions, and speeches, games and speeches. We declined, saying it was more important that we finished our work. So the villagers, faced with the choice of watching two foreigners twist wires together or going to the biggest party ever, made the logical choice. When Dan and I flipped the switch to illuminate the inside of the hut, we were the only two there to appreciate it.

We managed to get to the tail end of the party. The villagers ran up to us and heaped flower leis around our necks to honor us. We even got to hear a few speeches in Hindi. Then we met with members of the delegation and welcomed the new teacher they had brought to the school. He would provide eighty-one students with a new educational opportunity. We hoped that our lighting system would make it easier for the students to study. Our second hope was that the Light Up the World Foundation would follow up to light up more homes in this village.

Just before leaving we showed off the system to members of the village who would care for it, and then started the long hike back down the trail as the sun set.

Dan and I were relieved to have installed the system. Even packed in a tough box, we had worried that our destruction derby camels might damage the system before we could put it in place. Our other solar lighting systems were waiting for us in Nepal.

Dan mounts a solar panel into a frame the villagers helped us make. The frame was then mounted on a roof where water buffaloes would not damage it.

Looking for Tigers

Dan has a knack for making friends. He's a teddy bear-kind of guy who is interested in people. If someone has a skill, Dan will enthusiastically question them. Any new friend is the center of attention. While I was sick, Dan toured the park and met the local guides. He was so well received, the guides invited him home to meet their families. He sometimes had more dinner invitations than he could accept. Guide Deshraj Payla was especially helpful. After our hike to Dwar Mala I was healthy enough to look for tigers. Deshraj honestly told us he hadn't seen a tiger in four months.

"Finding a tiger is not easy," said Deshraj, "Especially after the recent rainstorms."

"Dan and I have been blessed or cursed," I said. "The rain gods have followed us across India."

"Rainstorms mean that the animals don't have to go to the major water holes and can get water all over the park."

"So we aren't going to just sit near a water hole and wait for a tiger to come to us?"

"Yes. To locate a tiger I use three techniques. First, we listen for the distress or warning calls of other animals such as sambar deer, monkeys, or birds. Second, we look for vultures." Deshraj pointed to the sky and circled a pointing finger. "Circling vultures may indicate a recent kill and a nearby tiger. Farmers lose about one water buffalo a week to a tiger in the park. Third, we look for tracks."

That day we followed a number of fresh tracks in hopes of finding a tiger. No luck. We did see sambar and spotted deer, a crocodile, several mongoose, nilgai, a fluorescent turquoise kingfisher, and many other species of birds.

The Sariska Tiger Reserve is part of Project Tiger, an effort to save India's dwindling tiger population. At the beginning of the 1900s, the tiger population of India was around 40,000. By 1972, the figure had dropped to 1,800.

"Deshraj, how many tigers are there in Sariska Park?" I asked.

"An interesting question. Ten years ago, our census showed over thirty tigers. The present count is twenty-seven."

"What is causing the tiger decline?"

"Maybe nothing."

"I don't follow."

"The way we counted tigers ten years ago was based on tiger sightings. The problem with sightings is whether you are looking at the same tiger. The new method combines sightings with taking plaster casts of the tracks. A cat track is something like a human fingerprint and can identify the big cats. So the Sariska Reserve has people go out whenever there is a sighting to make a cast to identify the tiger. While there seems to be a drop in numbers, this could be due to a more accurate counting technique. There may have been fewer tigers earlier."

Deshraj took us to where they kept the tiger footprint casts. There were large piles of casts. Once the casts were recorded they were discarded. I got several casts from a pile containing thousands made over the last ten years. The plaster cast would be as close as we got to seeing a tiger.

About this time, my wife, Ellen, eight-year-old son, Griffin, and two friends, Jim and Kathleen, flew to India. Keeping in touch via our satellite email and phone system, they hooked up with us at the Sariska Tiger Reserve. My wife was concerned when she saw me.

"What happened to you?" Ellen asked.

"I've lost some weight."

"Some weight! How much?"

Normally I weigh 200 pounds. "I'm down to a trim 165 pounds."

"Trim? More like you just got out of a concentration camp," she said worriedly.

To change the subject, I said, "Let's go find out what Dan and Griffin are up to."

We found them at the guides' compound, an area where park employees and their families live. Dan was introducing Griffin to the kids. He also introduced Griffin to India's sporting passion—cricket. While most Americans aren't familiar with the game of cricket, Indians are crazy about the game. It is the baseball, basketball, and football of India. Every village has an empty field where the children collect to play cricket in the evening. In the towns, men stop work to watch cricket matches on television. Others save for years to attend a live cricket match. Some of these games go on for five days. And I thought baseball innings went on forever.

The kids listened attentively to Dan as he explained a modified form of the game of cricket. Being from Britain, where cricket was invented, made Dan an instant expert. He had also become a bit of a hero to the children. He bonded with a youngster named Ravindra. Ravindra was a bright, polite, helpful contact, so we bought him a new cricket bat, ball, and stumps. Previously, the kids pooled all their rupees for a year to buy a new bat for the village. The bat they had when we arrived was a much-repaired piece of wood. The ball was ripped. The stumps consisted of some sticks. Their new equipment would improve their game playing. Soon Griffin was running, batting, leaping, and laughing with the other kids who all spoke Hindi while he spoke English. But they understood each other. Play is a universal language.

Jim with his wife, Ellen, son, Griffin, and camel, Sam. After introducing my family to our camels, we visited a nearby farm.

The Abandoned City

When Ashutosh heard that my family was visiting he called the hotel and left a message.

"I have something I came across here not long ago. It is a marvelous ruin. Would you be interested in visiting it? Not many tourists have been there. It's called the Abandoned City."

Ashutosh related the story of the Abandoned City as we drove out to the ruins. "A sorcerer wanted the queen of Bhangrah for his bride. So he mixed the ingredients for a magic potion. If the queen bathed her hair in the potion, she would fall under the sorcerer's spell and follow his commands. The potion was sent disguised as a gift. But the queen was also a witch. She recognized the gift for what it was. She cast her own spell and poured the potion onto a stone, which sprouted legs. Speaking to the stone, the witch said, "Find the sender of this gift and slay him." It hunted down the enchanter, and found him sitting in a small shrine that overlooks the city. There the enchanted stone carried out the queen's command. Before the magician died, he muttered a curse: 'Anyone who remains in the city past the setting of the sun will follow me in death.' The town folk were terrified. They left the city in a panic."

Castle walls surround the palace inside the Abandoned City.

Nine hundred years later, Bhangrah is still deserted. Locals run goats through the once-magnificent grounds during daylight, but as night approaches, everyone leaves. The curse still has power. Entering through a portal in the wall that once protected the city, we peeked into a temple at the gate. A tiny candle illuminated a spooky figure in the shadows. An eight-foot-high statue with a misshapen head painted blood red—the monkey god, Hanuman— glowered back at us from the gloom. Under his menacing gaze we entered the city.

A small shrine atop the hill to the left overlooks an intricately carved temple in the Abandoned City. Legend says that a dying magician cursed the city from this lofty point. Locals are still reluctant to venture into the city after nightfall.

A curved stone trail leads between symmetrical buildings that were once shops. Ancient temples covered with carvings point toward the heavens like fat skeletal fingers. Banyan trees hug the buildings with intertwined roots. Presiding over the town is a palace. It is backed up against cliffs that once formed a natural protective wall. Now monkeys chatter and leap where royalty once held court. Local legend has it that bags of gold and silver coins are hidden beneath the palace. We climbed into the palace. I thought I saw a monkey with what looked like a gold coin clutched in its hand, but the light was poor and I could have been mistaken.

A small open-air temple is perched on a rock outcrop high above the city. This is where the magician is reputed to have uttered the curse that resulted in the evacuation of the city.

"Dan," I said. "If we ever come back this way, I say we sleep in the cursed temple up there."

"You're on," said Dan.

Child Labor

Ashutosh had one more stop for us after the Abandoned City, a visit to the village of Ajabgarh. This village is part of a multimillion dollar business. Children as young as ten are part of the work force. The work is intricate, and a child's nimble fingers are an advantage. One hundred families are involved in the manufacture of hand-loomed carpets. The children sit at a loom that goes from floor to ceiling with hundreds of strands of string forming the weaving surface. Using dyed wool, they deftly slip a swatch in between the strings, snug it down, and cut it with a sharp curved knife. The finished carpet is rolled at the bottom of the loom.

I asked one of the villagers if I could squeeze into the working area and give it a try. They agreed, but took me to a loom being worked by women rather than twelve-year-old girls. They also made sure a man was seated between the veiled Hindu women and me. The man showed me how to pull out the correct strings in the pattern, wrap the wool, and then snug it down with a quick cut. It takes one person six to eight months to make one carpet, working eight-hour days. They showed us a picture of the carpet's design, but the weavers don't look at the pictures—both child and adult weavers have memorized the intricate pattern and work from memory. At the end of the workday, the children go to school at night. They are encouraged to attend classes by being provided free meals and books.

In the village of Ajabgarh, children learn how to weave carpets at a young age.

A six-by-nine-foot carpet that takes six or more months to make earns a rug-maker's family 5,000 to 6,000 rupees ($100 to $120 U.S.). This same carpet will sell in Europe or the United States for thousands of dollars. While the Indian government instituted laws in the early 1990s to prevent child labor, a provision of the law allows children to work in their homes. This allows the rug trade to provide an income to families that might otherwise have to rely on subsistence farming. Ashutosh had interviewed 1,800 families involved in making rugs in his district. He wanted to unite these families into a cooperative. As a cooperative, he believed that the villagers could reduce the huge amount of money taken by the middleman so that the weavers would receive more money for their efforts. This could translate into a better education for the children who are making these rugs. We were impressed by Ashutosh's efforts to improve the educational and other standards for the people he served.

Camel Criminals

It wasn't until near the end of our stay at Sariska that I found out about the camel criminals. The park has a livestock jail. Poachers sneak into the park to cut rare trees. The wood is loaded onto camels. Rather than take a chance of being caught with the goods, these tree poachers leave their loaded camels behind and slip out of the park. The camels behave like homing pigeons, instinctively heading back through the jungle towards home. When park rangers catch these illegal camel trains, the fine is a hefty 5,000 rupees ($100 U.S.) per camel—if the owners can be located. There were sixteen camel criminals in the holding pen as I walked by. This annoyed both Dan and me, who had been told there were no facilities for holding camels in the park.

The Negligent Farmer

Speaking of criminals, the park officials had ordered that our camels be stabled outside the immediate confines of the Sariska Reserve because there were no facilities for holding camels in the park. The officials recommended a farmer, Kaloo Ram, to watch over our camels. He proved to be a rotten choice. After making a surprise visit to check up on our camels, Dan returned to the hotel in a rage.

"That bloody farmer has completely botched our camels," ranted Dan.

"He's what?" I asked.

"Humper and GB are a mess," Dan heatedly explained. "That sod Kaloo is letting them run free in the bush. I figure they got their nose reins tangled around a branch. You know how they will yank on their lines till they get free." Dan was working himself up. He wanted to strangle Kaloo. "Last time I inspected the camels, I told him, 'Don't let the camels go free in the jungle.' Considering how much we are paying him, you'd think he'd listen. But when I went to check up on him today, the camels were wandering around again. Their noses are gutted. I told Kaloo that I'm bringing in a vet and I'm taking the money out of his wages."

When I got over my own health problems and went out to check on the camels, I agreed with Dan. We had some ill camels. Being around camels, you quickly learn to recognize the signs that indicate trouble. First, you see if the camel is in a munching mood. Camels get as much pleasure from chewing cud as a kid gets from chewing gum. The only time they stop chewing is when they are asleep, running, or sick. You can also inspect their poop. Solid golf-ball-sized pea-green poop is a thumbs-up dump for health. A camel under stress can change its pooping habit in minutes. I remember watching the stoic GB, afraid of nothing, suddenly get the runs when confronted with a two-foot-tall camel statue. Something about the sculpture terrified her. She bellowed and pulled away, her fear turning into instant diarrhea. We never figured out what made the statue so terrifying.

The camel statue that terrorized GB, yet our other camels showed no fear or interest in this dromedary sculpture.

I tallied up the damage to our camels. Sam had two broken nose pegs. GB and Humper's condition was more serious. They looked miserable and kept shaking their heads. I got a grip on GB and looked up her nostrils. I saw a mass of squirming larvae. I turned to Dan and said, "Maggots." Flies had laid eggs in GB's wounded snout. Humper had the same problem.

I agreed with Dan. We should dig a deep pit and bury Kaloo.

When the vet arrived he gave us his opinion.

"The camels will need medication and a week of rest. Then they should be fit to travel."

I shook my head at the vet's diagnosis. Even with the small amount of time we had been around camels, Dan and I knew they wouldn't heal in a week. More like a month.

Dan and I had a conference. "I don't want to make them suffer just so we can finish the trip," I said.

"We don't have enough time to let them heal," replied Dan thoughtfully. "End of expedition?"

"I don't think so. What do you say we continue the trip with just two camels? Other than two broken nose pegs, something we can fix, Sam's OK. And Raika's nose is made out of rock. GB and Humper are too sick to continue."

"I bet that bloody farmer let them get injured so that he could buy them cheap."

"You might be right. Let's call Bubbles and see what he advises."

As a supportive friend, Bubbles was amazing. Without hesitation, Bubbles drove all the way from Bikaner to Sariska. In the car with him were two camel men. Talking with them, we decided to send Humper and GB back to Bikaner by truck. We also discussed with Bubbles what we wanted done with the camels. After they healed we asked if he would sell them to good camel people.

Bubbles had pressing business back in Bikaner, so he turned around and drove back. Later we discovered that Bubbles was running for mayor of Bikaner. Even among all the politics and work of running for office, operating a hotel, building a second hotel, and running a number of other businesses, he was willing to help two friends on their crazy expedition.

The farmer paid to watch over our camels let them run wild in the jungle. This resulted in a number of broken nose pegs. Dan is replacing a nose peg on Sam. To prepare Sam for this delicate operation, her front legs were hobbled. Then a stout tree limb was tied to her halter and four people kneeled on the limb to hold the camel's head to the ground. Dan lubricated a new nose peg with mustard oil, which also acts as a disinfectant, and inserted it up a nostril into a slit in her nose. Even with all the precautions, Sam still yanked her handlers around.

The two camel men hitched a ride into Shapura to rent a truck and driver for transport of the camels. When they returned we started the loading process. First, we needed a steep embankment. An earthen dam was located nearby. The truck backed the tailgate up level with the dam. Then we shoveled dirt into the truck bed to pad the floor. GB walked docilely onto the truck bed and kneeled down where she was trussed up like a Thanksgiving turkey. Humper was less obliging. No amount of pulling, offerings of food, or cursing would induce her to enter the truck. That's when we saw the genius of practical experience. One of the camel men piled more dirt on the truck bed and tailgate. Then Humper was lured as close to the truck as she would come. Here she was made to kneel and her legs were hobbled. Then six of us pushed and shoved. Humper slid on the loose dirt, roaring her displeasure. But she ended up in the back of the truck trussed up next to GB. As the truck departed for Bikaner, I thought Dan might cry. He'd become fond of GB and was sad to see her go.

That's when Dan turned to confront the farmer. Our park guide and friend, Deshraj, helped to interpret some of the finer points we wanted to get across.

Dan started with, "You're a worthless sack of camel droppings. We were paying you well to watch our camels. We would have been better off letting them run wild."

I don't think Deshraj translated exactly what Dan said, because the farmer nodded and smiled back at us.

"We hold you responsible for the injuries to our camels. You were told not to let them run free in the jungle and ignored my request. I told you more than once. We are subtracting the vet payment from the 3,000 rupees we were going to pay you. The vet charged 600 rupees, that means you get 2,400."

The smile disappeared from the farmer's face, "You promise 3,000."

"*You* don't get it, do you?" fumed Dan. "You are lucky we don't charge *you* for the loss of two camels and the truck transport back to Bikaner."

"Give me all or nothing," complained the farmer.

"Fine, then nothing it is," finished Dan.

Mild-mannered Deshraj was caught in the middle as the interpreter. He did his best to calm both sides. I suspected some of what we said and some of what the farmer said was diplomatically translated to make it less harsh.

I held 2,400 rupees in my hand. Dan grabbed the reins for Sam and Raika and said, "Let's go. If the sod doesn't want the money, that's his problem."

As we walked away, the farmer's father, an elderly man who had been smoking a water pipe as he listened to the exchange, held a hurried conversation with his son. He probably said something like, "Don't be *stupid*. Take the money."

The farmer ran after us and held his hand out for the money.

I slapped the money on his open palm. No one said thank you.

The long layover in Sariska and our camel problems had seriously cut into our trip time. It was November 7, day 72 of the expedition. We had covered 250 miles and had 28 days left. Dan and I discussed our plans as we walked along.

"At the rate we are going," said Dan, "we aren't going to make it to Tibet. Even making it to Nepal seems pretty iffy. Plus we have the problem of the Maoist rebels threatening to kill tourists in Nepal."

"Remember when Iqrar said he thought we'd be lucky to make it to Agra?" I reminded Dan. "Let's shoot for Agra. I've got an idea how we can make it to Nepal, but let's see what happens with Agra first."

Camel Talk VI

Gone, thought Sam. GB and Humper gone. She felt herd loss. Camel law says that there is strength in the herd. That is why she had broken her tether on the first day in the strange city so many days ago. She had desperately wanted to catch up with GB and Raika who were going for a walk with the new food givers. She needed to stay with her herd—no matter how small it was. She wondered if Raika felt the same.

"Do you miss them?" asked Sam cautiously.

"Miss that worthless Humper?" said Raika scornfully. "You aren't serious?" She shook her head. "But GB is a loss. Now that she is gone, I have to carry the big food giver. He is the heaviest two-leg I've ever carried. If GB were here she could strain under his weight."

"It doesn't make you sad that our herd has lost?"

"Sad is weak. I leave that to you."

Sam didn't flinch. Raika's comments didn't sting like they had in the early days.

"There are weak camels and there are strong camels," lectured Raika. "When I tangled my reins in the jungle, I broke them. My nose was strong. That's why no maggots grew in my nostrils like they did in GB and Humper's snouts. Maggots live where there is weakness."

"I wonder what GB would have thought of your words," said Sam.

Raika waved her long neck and said, "It was only a matter of time before I showed GB who the herd leader was."

Sam wasn't able to control herself and said, "I noticed that the male camel that chased you the other day did not hear any such strong words. You hid behind your food giver. If not for his stick, the male would have had you."

"The male with tattoos covering his body," Raika trembled slightly. "I was surprised, that's all."

"When he ground his teeth together, you looked as if you would fall to the ground," said Sam. "You are fortunate that your food giver stood his ground."

For the first time in many days, Raika had no comment.

The punk camel look. Manes clipped into Mohawks, wearing red bandanas, and decorated by their owners with tattoos, male camels not only looked menacing but could be dangerously aggressive. These bad boys showed a lot of interest in our female camels. Standing your ground when one of these slobbering demons ran towards our little caravan was always an unnerving experience.

On To Agra

With only two camels, we needed to strip our gear down to the minimum. We kept:

- tents
- a change of clothing
- cameras
- two blankets
- ground pads
- first aid kit
- jackets
- journals
- water bottles
- water purification equipment
- satellite phone
- headlamps
- Gerber multitool
- money
- Dan's bear

All my gear fit into one small duffle bag and a blanket roll. It looked like I was going to the gym to work out rather than riding across India. We packed our camels using a pattern seen in an old photo of an Indian camel soldier, bag on the front of the saddle, blanket roll lashed to the back. Fortunately, we had planned to pick up additional solar lighting systems in Nepal for the Nepal and

Tibet legs of the trip rather than carry them through India. That meant we could get rid of the bulky protective boxes used to transport the solar panels and other delicate gear. Minimal equipment cut down our morning packing time from an hour to ten minutes.

Payback

Now there would just be four of us—Dan, Jim, Raika, and Sam. I got Sam. Dan got Raika. And I got payback. Earlier in the trip, Dan had joked about my camel-handling skills. This was when he was riding the mature, sensible, predictable GB while I dealt with tantrum-prone, harebrained, schizophrenic Raika. I'm sure Dan's comments were made in jest, but they rankled none the less.

Now it was Dan's turn to discover why I called Raika *pagal hai* (crazy). I have fond memories of Dan gripping the sissy bar on Raika's saddle and wildly galloping off in the opposite direction of our destination. Then there is the memory of Dan's bobbing head, just visible above a field of cotton plants, chasing the bobbing head, neck, and hump of Raika. In this chase Raika had both of her front legs tied together and yet she still outran Dan. My all-time favorite is when Raika pretended to be the tornado in *The Wizard of Oz*. On this occasion Dan was dumped on the ground clutching two broken reins. Playfully, Raika took off, pursued by a cursing Dan. I tried following, but soon lost sight of them. Sometime later, Dan appeared seated on the back of a motorcycle. He'd made it to a road and asked a motorcyclist to help with the chase. Dan was roaring down the highway shouting encouragement to the driver as Raika loped up the road ahead of them. When Raika saw Sam, she veered off the road down the slope and sauntered up to stand calmly next to us. I looped a rope around her neck. Dan was not amused.

As Dan approached, he said in a matter-of-fact way, "I'm going to kill that barmy twit of a camel."

I impressed myself with my restraint. This was my chance to take a dig at Dan's camel-handling skills. Instead I said sympathetically, "How do you plan on doing it?"

"I think I'll spit her and roast her alive. Turn her into camel burgers."

Raika looked totally unconcerned. Dan slipped a bamboo rod out of his saddle. He had showed considerable restraint up to this point. I gave him some advice. "I've heard that abused camels have been known to unexpectedly turn on their owners and kill them."

Dan mulled this over and lowered the stick. Then he vented his anger with creative verbal insults. "A dead cow has more brains. She's as useless as a chocolate teapot. If the traffic doesn't kill her, I will." All said in the sweetest of voices.

These camel crises were humorous—but only afterwards. During the bucking-out-of-control moments, Dan and I could only watch each other with a certain dread and hope that things would turn out all right. It was a matter of trusting our karma.

Some days we pushed our karma to the limit.

"Dan, want to make some distance today?" I asked. "Let's ride at a full gallop as long as we can get them to go."

"If you can stay in front of me, you're on," said Dan.

The problem would be to keep Sam in front of Raika. As long as Raika was chasing another camel, she'd be controllable. Once she got past that camel, you never knew where she would veer. That meant Dan would have to rein in Raika as she could easily outrun Sam.

I hissed, "Jai, jai," the command to kneel, and Sam dropped to the ground. Dan did the same with Raika. We mounted with a sense of excitement. As Sam rose I tapped her thighs and we started galloping down a dirt road. Never one to be left behind, Raika lunged off the ground and came in pursuit. Riding a running camel is white-knuckled excitement. A running camel can get up to 30 miles per hour. Bobbing along eight feet above the ground, Dan and I whooped as the camels sprinted along the track. As we rocketed past emerald-green fields, women dressed in crimson saris rose up to watch us pass. Several men raised their hands to shade their eyes and shouted greetings. I'm sure they wondered where we had come from and where we were vanishing to. Sprinting along next to Dan, both of us yelling "*Yee-haa!*" and grinning like we'd won the lottery, is one of my fondest adrenalin-engraved memories of the trip.

At this point we found a road that didn't show on our Indian road atlas. The farms were bigger. In the early part of the trip, the plots were small enough that a farmer could see all of his land from his front porch. Now we traveled by big fields of cotton and onions without a house in sight.

Camel carts hauling huge loads of cotton were a common sight. Even the vehicles were memorable. Some cars reminded us of movies. There was a three-wheeled parrot-nosed vehicle from *Mad Max*. Dan's favorite truck had a grill covered with bells and ornaments, and was overloaded like something from the "Beverly Hillbillies."

Shrines, Shrines Everywhere

A religious shrine to the god Shiva. One of the many we saw during the trip.

Religious shrines cover India. They are more common than telephone poles. One night we found a hidden spot in a grove of trees. Tucked between the trees was a shrine glowing with the last rays of the setting sun against a dappled backdrop of shadows. The mini-temple was capped with a trident indicating it was dedicated to Shiva, one of the Hindu gods. Shiva is sometimes depicted surrounded by serpents, wearing a skull necklace, and using one of his four arms to brandish a trident. That night it felt like he was plunging his trident into my thighs. Both my legs cramped after a full day of walking.

Having been a competitive swimmer, I was familiar with run-of-the-mill calf cramps, but these cramps were something else. It felt like being electrocuted. My inner legs spasmed from ankle to groin. I twisted, turned, and stretched, trying to stand up to release the terrible tension. The only thing that helped was forcing a state of relaxation. Trying to go limp. A lack of potassium can cause cramping. Bananas are a good source of potassium. So the following morning I ate a King Kong helping of bananas. Sam didn't look pleased that I was stealing her food.

Swastikas

The first time I saw a swastika on the trip, I did a double take. Swastikas, the sign of Hitler's Germany, were painted on tall chimneys spewing smoke. It looked like pictures I'd seen of Auschwitz, the horrible German death camp of World War II, only these chimneys indicated the presence of a brick works, not a death camp. Well maybe in a way it is a death camp—for the soul. Making bricks is a harsh job. The clay for the bricks is dug out of the ground next to the tall smokestacks. Each brick is then hand formed and baked in the ovens below the chimneys. After a mind-numbing day of digging clay, hand-packing bricks into molds, and carrying bricks back and forth between the ovens, workers retire to their housing.

A tall smokestack indicates a brick factory. Soil from the surrounding area is compacted into rectangular molds to shape bricks. These clay bricks are then baked in an oven to complete the process.

The workers' housing is a reminder of their job. It is part brick-storage yard and part shanty. The bricks are stacked into temporary walls. Sheets of corrugated metal are laid on top of these brick boxes for roofs. These are the brick workers' homes. The swastika symbol has none of the stigma in India that it has in the West. In India it is a sign of good luck. Though if you work in a brick works, I don't think you are very lucky.

The Swastika

The swastika symbol was used in the Hindu religion long before it was adopted by Hitler's Germany. In the Hindu religion it is a sacred icon. Indians put the swastika on everything from cake decorations to the entrance to a house. Nazi Germany's use of the swastika gave it a new meaning associated with evil.

Noises at Night

As the sun approached the horizon, we came to a military base. A large block wall, the outer perimeter barbwired, watch towers, and guarded entrances stretched off into the distance. We wanted to get by the wall before setting up camp, but the wall seemed endless. We trudged along its perimeter. It got darker and darker. By the time we reached the end of the wall, the stars had come out. Crossing a bridge, I looked down on a dry riverbed. A dry riverbed is a good indicator of possible campsites.

We steered our camels down the embankment and walked up the riverbed. In a short time, we came to a strange feature in the channel: a stadium-sized bowl fifty yards in diameter. The banks were fifteen feet high, fringed with man-high pampas grass. The bottom of the bowl was covered with fine sugar-white sand. It was unnaturally level, as if someone had smoothed it with a ruler.

"What do you think it is?" I asked.

Dan pivoted around, "Maybe a nuclear subsurface test site."

"I'm thinking an alien landing zone. Just right for flying saucers."

"It's as flat as a firing range."

"I don't have a clue," I said. "But I don't see any scorpion plant and any place without scorpion plant is a good place to camp. Let's use the pampas grass to tie up the camels."

While setting up our tents, a tractor came in with its lights blazing. Blinded by the light, Dan tried to explain we were camping. They left.

Settled into our tents for the night, I thought I'd have a chance to catch up on my journal writing without having local villagers collect around our tents like moths attracted to a flame. It turned out that it would get much more exciting this evening. As I wrote, I thought I heard a noise, a cough, some rustling. I told Dan to turn out his light as I clicked off mine.

Moments later, a shout came from the bank above. It was in Hindi. I had no idea what was said. A spotlight clicked on, illuminating our campsite. More shouting followed. I started putting my shoes on, calling back in Hindi, *Ek minit* (one minute). The shouting got louder and more angry. I called back, *Nahii mai samjaha hindi. Angrezi atti hai?* (I don't understand Hindi. Do you speak English?).

That's when the voice shifted to English. "Get out of your tents now. We have guns and will shoot!"

That got me moving. Then the voice said, "Throw out your weapons!"

As I exited the tent, I said, "We don't have any weapons." I heard bolts being pulled back on rifles. Dark figures dotted the ridgeline silhouetted by the starry night sky. I could see the barrels of rifles.

The voice was angry, "Where are the other people?"

"There aren't any other people," I called back.

He repeated the question, "Where are the other people?"

"There aren't any others," I insisted. "Who are you?"

He ignored my question, "Put your hands on your head or we will shoot."

There wasn't much I could do but put my hands on my head. Dan, in the meantime, was struggling in his tent to get some clothing on. (Dan sleeps naked while I often slept fully clothed so I could move at a moment's notice.)

Coming out of my tent I faced a ridge dotted with the silhouettes of heads and guns. The guns were aimed at me.

The angry voice yelled, "Get the other people out of the tent or we will shoot into the tent."

"There's only me and my friend," I said as calmly as I could. "Dan, I think you better get out here now."

"I'm bloody well trying to get my pants on," snapped Dan.

"Dan," I said urgently, "I think this may be a choice between modesty and a bullet."

Dan came out trying to pull up his pants.

The angry voice demanded, "Put your hands up or we shoot."

Dan reluctantly put his hands up as his pants began to slide down. Then men in full camouflage gear and grease-painted faces started sliding down the embankment around us. Who were these guys?

There were guns all over the place. I was particularly impressed by the machine gun aimed at my head. It looked like the Tommy guns used by mobsters back in the 1920s. We were surrounded. Dan's pants in the meantime slid to half-mast. He asked for permission to lower his hands to pull them up. The angry voice walked up shining a spotlight in my face.

We were surrounded. One of the guns pointed at me looked like a Thompson submachine gun. Dan's pants kept slipping down as he tried to comply with the command to keep his hands behind his head.

The questions came rapidly. "Who are you?" "Where are you from?" "Where did you get the camels?" "Where are your guides?"

Finally he said, "We were told that you threatened local farmers with guns. They said armed Afghan or Kashmiri terrorists were camped out in their field."

"Inspect our tents," I offered. "We don't have any weapons. There aren't any other people. No guides. It's just me, Dan, and our two camels. We didn't threaten anyone." While they inspected our meager possessions, Dan and I talked rapidly, explaining our adventure, camels, BBC, and journalist status. It took awhile before the leader told his men to lower their weapons. He was beginning to accept that we weren't terrorists.

Perpetual journalist that I am, I asked, "Can I take a photo of you and your men?"

"We are a special military unit," he replied stiffly. "There will be no photos, no information about the base, and no names."

Dan couldn't resist. He said, "We understand. Thank you, Captain _____," using the captain's name.

The captain was immediately on guard and asked sternly, "How did you know my name?"

"It's on the patch above your pocket," said Dan.

The captain looked self-consciously at his sewn-in nametag. I rolled my eyes at Dan. I think at that point the captain recognized the ridiculousness of the situation. Here, minutes before, he had a full SWAT team aiming machine guns at two harmless foreigners: one with his trousers halfway down, no weapons, hardly any gear, obviously not terrorists. The tension eased as he smiled and asked, "Have you had tea?"

As we waited for tea, he asked me to explain to his men the details of our adventure-education-charitable mission. The assault team that had been aiming rifles at us moments before were now seated on the sand in a kindergarten half-circle listening to my improvised lecture.

The captain told one of the soldiers to go collect the people who had accused us of being terrorists. They were the farmers on the tractor who had seen us earlier. You don't see foreigners in this area very often, especially on camels. It was our strangeness that convinced them we were up to no good. When they were informed of their error, they were embarrassed and to apologize, they brought dinner for us. Spreading out the food on a tarp, Dan and I had our second meal of the evening.

The captain pulled out a cell phone. "I need to tell my wife that everything is OK so she won't worry." After speaking for a few minutes, he turned to Dan, "Would you say a few words to her?"

Dan took the phone and said a few pleasantries.

"Thank you," said the captain. "You have made our night memorable. I apologize for the misunderstanding. The Indian army never wants to appear to be a bully or unfair. Our response was only because we thought there was a threat. Is there anything that the Indian military can do to help you?"

I thought for awhile and said, "Tomorrow we have to get through the city of Bharatpur. It's a big town and sometimes we have trouble with the camels on busy streets."

"Tomorrow," said the captain, "I will personally come and give you a military escort through town."

The next morning Dan and I took advantage of the soft sand in the riverbed. The camels could always use a little more training. We took turns mounting up and riding around the arena. Sam was not interested. Even though Raika had acted like Sam's wicked stepsister, taking every opportunity to bite and bully her, Sam didn't want to leave Raika's side and spiraled back towards her, no matter what I did to try to direct her. At one point Sam tired of my steering. She started bucking wildly. I didn't have my sissy handle strap set up and felt myself lift into the air. Events slow down when I'm in trouble. Sam camelpulted me into the air, an out-of-control aerial dismount. I was flying parallel to the ground. I clearly saw one foot fly out of the stirrup, but the other was still stirruped. It snapped through my mind that this trapped foot would get me dragged across the arena. As if in slow motion, I pointed my toe and pulled my foot free. Then things speeded up. I hit the ground flat on my back, *Whoompfh*. Laying there I checked for broken bones. Luckily there was no damage.

Not long after my flying lesson, the captain arrived to escort us.

"Did you have a good rest?" he asked.

"Other than some late night visitors," said Dan cheekily, "it was the bee's knees."

"What he means," I translated, "is yes."

The captain eyed the camels and their saddles. "Do you think I might ride one of the camels?"

Dan and I looked at each other. The same thing was going through our minds.

"Sure," said Dan. "Let's use Raika. Sam is a little jumpy this morning."

As Raika rose up with the captain on her back, Dan held the reins firmly and started to lead her.

"Could I not ride by myself without you holding the reins?" asked the captain.

Dan shook his head. "I don't think that would be a good idea."

After riding, the captain guided us on a route around the outskirts of Bharatpur. This particular day was a religious holiday. Even though the captain could have spent the holiday with his family, he said, "It is not often that I get to meet two adventurers. There will be other holidays. It is my pleasure to help you."

He asked many questions. One of the questions was the one that journalists all over India had asked us, "Why the camels?"

"They are keys," I replied.

"Keys?"

"If we came to India as tourists in an air-conditioned bus, we wouldn't see India. It would be like watching a movie through the glass windows. Our camels help the Indian people view us less as tourists. The camels have opened up the hospitality and the lives of people we meet. For example, if we pass a camel cart and greet the driver with *Ram-ram,* the driver looks over our camels. Then there's a smile. That smile says, you have camels, you understand some of my life. Then he pats the back of the cart, an offer to ride along with him. Sitting on bags of cotton, Raika and Sam trotting along behind the cart, we share conversation with the driver."

As the captain left us on the other side of the city he said, "I am amazed you have made it this far. Camels, desert, bandits—be very careful. The next leg of your journey is even more dangerous."

You Are Very Beautiful

Even mundane tasks are interesting on an expedition—such as bathing. To clean off the day's grimy sweat, we bathed in the out- flow of irrigation pipes, showered under field sprinklers, and Jacuzzied in irrigation ditches. Usually we bathed like the locals next to a hand pump. Stripped down to boxer shorts we pumped water into cans that we poured over our heads. This was also a good time to wash clothing. It took less than a half-hour for cloth- ing to dry in the hot sun. During one of our bathing stops under a pump, a boy on a bike stopped to watch the show. In English, he commented, "You are very beautiful." I wasn't sure how to take this comment. While my wife and son were visiting India, people had come up to my wife and told her she was very beautiful. It put a big smile on her face. Then they stood there uncomfortably and asked, "Are you man or woman?" Her short hair, slacks, and lack of makeup confused them. I told Dan I would take the praise literally, but more likely it meant my appearance was unique and thereby interesting, like some exotic zoo animal.

Regardless of the intention, I took advantage of the situation, "Can I borrow your bike?" He looked surprised. In a show of trust he wheeled the bike over and offered me the handlebars. I hopped onto the bike holding Sam's reins. Riding in circles, Sam surprised me by following the bike, a device that had spooked her at the beginning of the trip.

Indian Bicycles

Indians are more likely to own a bicycle than a car. These are big, clunky, single-geared bikes—one size fits all. If a kid was too small to reach the pedals from the seat of his adult-sized two-wheeler, he stuck a leg through the frame to reach the pedals and then leaned the bike at an angle to counterbal- ance his weight. If this didn't seem awkward enough, some of these little kids carried thirty-gallon cans of water buffalo milk on their leaning bikes. Heavily loaded bicycles were a common sight. Cyclists passed us transporting television-sized cartons and quilts stacked six feet high. Some pedalers balanced loads of sugar cane stalks across their frames that took up the entire road, sort of like a teeter-totter with the bike in the middle. Other riders transported long steel pipes by strapping the pipe to their bike frame. Ten feet of pipe protruded from the front and back of these bicycles like the lances of medieval jousters. This was a serious hazard for inattentive pedestrians or foreigners with camels.

Dan and I discussed buying bikes. We could ride a bike while towing the camels behind. Used bikes cost 500 rupees ($10 U.S.). It would be a change of pace. The idea was discarded when Dan tried towing Raika. She almost yanked him off the back of the bike.

Dan tests out a bicycle while towing a camel.

Getting yanked was a real danger because we were now into Diwali, the Indian version of Christmas. Incendiary devices are a big part of this celebration. Town streets are lined with arsenals of fireworks vendors. They don't sell your harmless Fourth of July sparklers. This is the stuff of the U.S. national anthem—rockets red glare, bombs bursting in air. We worried that *goras* (foreigners) might be a target for a festive cherry bomb or rocket launched star burst. Who knew what damage our camels might do if spooked by friendly fire? We wanted to be far from a town when we camped.

We found a small family temple several miles from the city. The local farmer said we were welcome to stay the night. Sitting with our backs against a shrine, we watched the fireworks light up the sky from the distant town. Tomorrow we hoped to reach a really big town, Agra.

The Eighth Wonder of the World

Our contact in Agra was Gopal Singh. Bubbles had provided us with his name. On our satellite phone, Gopal agreed to arrange a place to stay for both the camels and us. The Laurie Hotel was our target.

The streets of Agra were congested with jostling people and traffic. The pedestrians weren't used to seeing camels on the street. In other towns, close to the desert and camels, people ignored us or reluctantly moved to the side at our approach. Here, people scrambled out of the way when they saw our dromedaries. Raika and Sam were also better behaved. They were more used to the commotion.

I waved down an autorickshaw driver. He looked confused when I tried to hire him.

He pointed at the camels and back to his vehicle, "Camels no fit."

"We don't want you to take the camels," I said.

"Do you wish a ride?" he asked. Then quickly added, "But what will you do with the camels?"

"No," I replied. "I don't want a ride. The camels don't want a ride."

"Then what do you wish, sahib?" he asked, looking puzzled.

"Do you know the Laurie Hotel?"

"Yes."

"We want to hire you to guide us there. You need to drive slowly. Keep us in view and we will follow you."

Understanding spread across his face. He nodded enthusiastically and leaped back into his putt-putt.

We were in for a surprise when we arrived at the hotel. The desk clerk took one look at our camels and tried to shoo us away. "No camels are allowed here."

I thought, *Here we go again*. "You don't understand. Gopal Singh called for us and arranged for our camels to stay here."

"I know nothing of a Gopal Singh or camels. You must leave."

I refused to budge and insistently asked for the manager.

The manager was equally befuddled by our camels. "We don't accept camels."

"Weren't you contacted by Gopal Singh?" I asked. "He said you had agreed to put us up."

"I've not been contacted by anyone about your staying here."

"You mean you didn't hear about the press conference that we hoped to hold at your hotel?" I asked. "We've ridden all the way from Bikaner and many newspapers and television stations want to hear our story." The Sariska Tiger Reserve had taught us the importance of publicity. Especially if the establishment we were staying at got some of that free publicity.

"A press conference?" he said. "At the hotel?"

He signaled we should be given a room and our camels could be tied up outside. He even made arrangements for a gardener to collect camel food for us. This was again a lesson on the importance of speaking to the person in charge if you want something done. Everyone else wants to keep life simple and avoid the unusual.

The next morning we visited India's most famous national treasure—the Taj Mahal. It was built by a grieving Mughal Emperor. His wife died when giving birth to their fourteenth child. Like the pyramids of Egypt, it is a giant tombstone. It is listed as the eighth Wonder of the World. Indian officials are lobbying to get the Taj moved up to the seventh wonder. Apparently being seventh or eighth is a big deal for tourism. This change could be a problem considering that the original list of seven was made by a scholar from the fifth century BCE who is unlikely to change his mind.

To me, the Taj is part of an elusive mystery. Every day you see men clothed in garments so white, it looks like angels dropped robes from heaven. Yet the water used to wash this clothing comes from rivers and streams the consistency and color of tea. This mystery extends to the Taj Mahal. The structure glowed pure white above a city smothered by air and water pollution. Inspecting the

Taj carefully, I saw metal rings embedded in the circumference of
the dome. Were these rings used to support secret midnight clean-
ers? How it stays so white is a miracle, but this façade of whiteness
is being eaten away. The level of sulfurous and nitrous compounds
in the air (smog from auto exhaust and industry) creates acid rain
that is devouring the marble and sandstone that make up the buildings. Monitors on the monument indicated that the danger level is
exceeded on a regular basis. A nearby workyard contained slabs of
fresh sandstone. They were being carved to duplicate portions of
the surrounding structure that had dissolved away like sugar in a
rainstorm. Given enough time, the whole building may eventually
be replaced with repair parts.

The first thing I noticed on the grounds of the Taj were the
reflecting pools. They actually had water in them. Most of the pal-
aces and museums we had seen with fountains, intricate channels,
and pools were bone dry. Even more amazing, the water in the
reflecting pools was clean. I wanted to jump in. But a man paced
back and forth, blowing on a whistle to move people away from the
pools. It was a futile job, like trying to make a hole in water. The
people just flowed in behind him. I think the tigers we failed to see
at the Sariska Tiger Reserve should be chained to posts around the
pools to ward off disobedient tourists.

To enter the Taj, religious conventions require that you
remove your shoes. The feeling of bare feet on polished marble
was deliciously cool. Of course there are so many bare feet, the
cleanliness of this practice is questionable. Enterprising vendors
offered to encase tourists' shoes in clean room booties. We were
told the reason you aren't allowed to wear shoes on the floor is
because shoes are made of cowhide, cows are sacred, and a dead
cow's skin would desecrate the shrine.

While the Taj is viewed as an architectural wonder, I'd personally make some changes. The entrance leading into the dome of the
building isn't much wider than the door to my bathroom at home.
Daily, thousands of tourists struggle to get into the inner sanctum
through this narrow opening while thousands more fight to get
out. It is a groping gauntlet of stranger intimacy. Even Dan and I,

with our combined 365 pounds of linebacker weight, had trouble pushing through the forget-politeness mob. In the melee of getting inside, one sari-clad grandmother repeatedly elbowed me in the ribs, smiling up at me as she did it. I was sorely tempted to poke back at her.

The Taj Mahal, eighth wonder of the world, trying hard to move up to position number seven.

Agra also provided another chance for media coverage. At a press conference, with a bank of ten microphones, TV cameras rolling, and an assembly of newspaper reporters, we answered questions. The big question was how two foreigners who don't speak the language, don't know the terrain, and know little about camels were able to make it from Bikaner to Agra. To them we were the *pagal gora* (crazy foreigners). One of the bigger news services then said they wanted to film Dan, the camels, and me with the Taj Mahal in the background. This meant we'd have to cross the city. With an autorickshaw leading the way, Dan and I, who had become considerably more adept at handling the camels in heavy traffic, set off on a dash across town to beat the setting sun. Television crews set up along the way recorded our passage. We posed in front of the Agra Fort and then made our way to the Yamuna River. With the Taj Mahal in the background seeming to float in a mist rising from the river, we participated in yet another interview as the sun set. Reuters news service picked up the photo and spread it across their international wire.

At the end of the interview, the photographers and journalists abandoned us. As twilight descended, Dan and I headed back towards the hotel. To keep from being hit by evening traffic, we hugged the side of the road. Hugging the road edge meant we were forced to walk on a white talcum powder-like substance. This isn't the kind of talc you would want to use on your baby's buns. It is a poison. This powder is sprinkled by street sweepers along the edge of roads. When it rains, the poison washes into sewers and pooling gutter water to kill mosquitoes. It's a preventative measure against malarial mosquitoes. We hoped walking on it wouldn't affect foreigners and their camels the same way it affected mosquitoes.

Traveling through the darkness, I mused on how the Silk Road had turned into the asphalt road. Our difficulty in riding camels across India was magnified by having to stick to roads. Riding cross-country in this area was not an option. Everything was farmed, fenced, ditched, and controlled. While silk suggests a soft landing if you are thrown from a disobedient camel, the asphalt suggests a hard landing in front of a lorry carrying a building-sized load of cane sugar. Fifty years ago it would have been easier to take camels through this area. Now it was like traveling through a hazardous arcade game. This camel route would only become more difficult with time.

Whenever Dan and I got to a big town we made up for all the meals we missed on the road. Even though Agra was a big town, we still took precautions with the food. At a fair in an upscale part of the city, vendors were selling food on the street. There was a big crowd of people buying food. To clean the cooking utensils, the cooks laid the pans out in the gutter. The flies buzzed heavily as dogs and cows licked the pans clean. We ate somewhere else.

Over dinner, we talked about our next goal.

"Back at Sariska, I'd mentioned I had a plan for making it to Nepal," I said.

"I remember," said Dan. "What do you have in mind?"

"Rather than follow our original route east across India and then turn up at the southern end of Nepal towards Katmandu, let's head north toward the western border of Nepal. It's shorter."

"Still sounds like a long shot, we've only got about two weeks left," said Dan.

"I know, but it would take us to another landmark, the Holiest of Rivers, the Ganges."

Thinking about the rumor that people were betting on how far we would make it, Dan smiled, "If people want to gamble, let's make sure that as many as possible who bet against us will lose their money."

We left Agra mid afternoon. The autorickshaw driver who had originally led us into town was hired to lead us out. Up to this point, I had dealt with most of my camel frustrations in a reasonable manner. But this was the day I lost it. I once took a seminar from Daniel Goleman, author of *Emotional Intelligence*. He explained that when we lose it, it is due to a brain hijacking. A portion of the brain, labeled the "amygdala," hijacks the rational part of the brain and takes over. The amygdala is described as being the size and shape of an almond. The nut descriptor is appropriate as it is the part of your brain that makes you nutty. When the amygdala takes over, you are as rational as a lizard and have the emotional sensitivity of a *Tyrannosaurus Rex*.

On a busy street, I was being dragged alongside Sam. She didn't like it when Raika led. It was as if she feared being left behind. When you are holding the reins at a camel's head you have the appearance of control, but when you drift back near the body, the balance favors the camel. Rushing ahead, Sam bumped me out into traffic. A car swerved, narrowly missing me. That's when my brain got hijacked. I yanked back on the reins and took a whack at Sam with my bamboo walking stick. To avoid me, she stumbled back-wards. Suddenly the look of reproach on her face changed to fear. Half of Sam disappeared into the ground. She'd backpedaled into a vertical shaft, an open storm drain. I watched in dismay as she scrabbled for purchase. I snatched her halter and leaned back to keep her from sliding further in. With her front leg drive and my leaning weight she struggled up out of the gaping hole. We both stood there staring at each other, a little shocked at the close call. As I surveyed the scene, I realized just how close a call. She could have slipped all the way down into the narrow shaft. She had also narrowly missed a jagged piece of pipe, a lone tooth in front of the gaping hole. A foot further over, and her 1,200 pounds would have been impaled on the stake. After checking Sam for broken bones, I breathed a heavy sigh and mentally berated myself for the next ten minutes. Aristotle said, "Anyone can become angry—that is easy. But to be angry—to the right degree, at the right time, for the right purpose, and in the right way—that is hard." On an anger manage-ment level I had blown it, but I figured the gods were watching. It was a cheap lesson. The consequences could have been much worse.

After our close call, I promised Sam I'd be more calm and asked for forgiveness. She nuzzled me.

Our minicaravan worked its way through the city, dealing with the normal hectic traffic. Then we arrived at a bridge. It was packed with slow-moving vehicles. No big trucks or buses were allowed on the bridge, but it was jammed with autorickshaws, cars, motorbikes, ox carts, donkey carts, and our two terrified camels. Inching along I looked down through a foot-wide gutter at the river below. The opening was big enough for a camel foot to slip into. Then we had an unexpected shock. Unknown to us, the top of the bridge was spanned by a railroad track. The bridge began to shake as a train clacked over the space above us. A month before we would have lost our camels. They would have leaped over the side rails and plunged into the water forty feet below. As it was, we barely managed to keep them on the bridge.

When we finally reached the other side of the bridge, our autorickshaw driver had a surprise waiting for us. At one of the many points where we lost sight of him in the crowd, he'd picked up a passenger. His fare hunched out of the autorickshaw and walked back to shake hands with us. I instinctively stepped back. The man's nose was missing. The hand he held out was minus a few fingers. His skin was pocked and mottled with white spots. He had leprosy, a bacterial disease that chews through an infected person's body parts. My knowledge of leprosy consisted of reading a single chapter in the book *Papillon*. In the book a convict, Papillon, tried to escape from Devil's Island by taking refuge in a leper colony. One of the lepers offered him a cigar from his diseased lips. Papillon smoked it, and the leper asked, "How did you know I had dry leprosy?" (Apparently dry leprosy isn't as contagious as wet leprosy.) Papillon replied, "I didn't." Well we didn't know either. Quick thinking Dan diplomatically explained that Europeans don't shake hands but bow and say "Namaste" if they hope to see someone again. Taking Dan's cue, I quickly bowed affirming that this was also an American custom. We hurriedly paid the autorickshaw driver, taking care to avoid touching his hands.

Tongas

At this point, our best day had been twenty miles. A twenty-mile day left little time for finding camel food, human food, or setting up camp. We realized that we needed a faster way to make time. This is when we remembered how much distance we traveled on a camel cart. Maybe we could rent one of the fast horse-drawn carts called *tongas*. Our camels could be towed along like house trailers to make up for lost time. For 400 rupees ($8 U.S.) we hired a tonga.

The horse didn't like the deal. One glimpse of the camels and the horse started pogo-sticking all over the place. The owner struggled to keep his pony from running off without us. To quiet the horse down, the owner wrapped a shawl around the horse's head so that he wouldn't see the camels. Then we loaded all our gear, except for the saddles, onto the cart. Legs dangling over the back of the cart, towing our two trotting girls, we covered twelve miles in a fraction of the time it had taken with the camels alone.

We hired a *tonga*, horse-drawn cart, to give us a ride while towing our camels behind the wagon. This horse had blinders, which proved to be a necessity. Animals this far north had never seen a camel and would dash away at first sight.

We had found a way to make good time, but we also lost something. During the early part of our journey, when we felt time rich, we'd take side trips whenever we saw something interesting. As our deadline approached, we started skipping interesting side trips, and measured our success in distance covered. We passed men crouched over a bucket with eels flopping out onto the ground, a burning funeral pyre, and women floating on a pond in half fifty-five-gallon drums collecting plants, but in our rush to "make it" we didn't stop to find out their stories. Instead, we reveled in each additional mile like misers over yet another gold coin. In many ways, this was less satisfying. It was like going on vacation with your parents and they won't stop at Disneyland just so they can make it to the state border before evening.

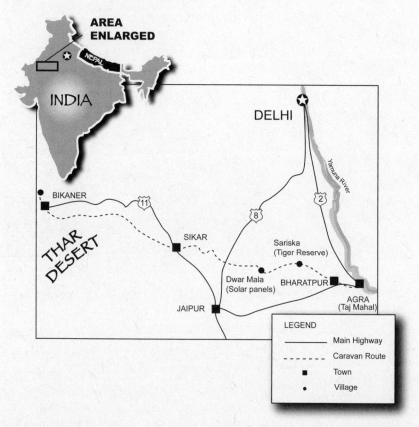

Bikaner to Agra is a distance of approximately 560 kilometers.

The Holiest of Rivers

Approaching the Ganges we saw huge "dung factories." Crouching women were busy turning livestock manure and straw into Frisbee-sized platters. To dry, these "manure Frisbees" were leaned one against another like cascading dominos frozen in time. But there was an art to it. Rather than stack them in practical library rows, there were patterns of circles and swirls. These designs covered many acres. It was like the Nazca lines in Peru, where prehistoric artists laid rocks in the outlines of strange figures that covered football field-sized areas. The

Manure Frisbees drying in the sun.

full artistry of the Nazca lines can only be appreciated by flying over the diagrams. It would be equally interesting to fly over this manure art. Later we discovered the purpose of the patties.

We made it to the Ganges River. As we prepared to cross the bridge, the guards told us, "No pictures!" The military is sensitive about bridges and does not allow photos. The pictures wouldn't have been very good anyway. A dense hazy smoke hung in the air. The smoke came from burning bodies. The Ganges is a cremation site. People travel from all over India with their deceased loved ones. They believe that having your ashes scattered upon the Ganges' sacred waters helps guarantee your chances of a better afterlife. It is considered the holiest of rivers.

The cremation process is simple. First a truck delivers firewood. The wood is laid out in a box pattern. Then those "manure Frisbees" are piled over the wood. The shroud-covered body arrives in the back of a large truck. The size of the truck bed allows mourners to squeeze in with the deceased. The shrouded body is then placed on the pyre and ignited. Dan and I watched from a respectful distance. Some of the mourners had their heads shaved by priests as a sign of mourning. Garlands of flowers were draped over the body, and songs were sung as holy men led the mourners through the ceremony. We were seated on a grassy field overlooking the river. Horses and water buffalo grazed the field. Several human skulls stared back at us. If a family did not have enough money to buy sufficient wood and cow dung cakes to burn the body, the remains were thrown into the river. Where we were seated, just above the river shoreline, there was a scattering of ribs, skulls, tibias, femurs, and pelvises being picked over by dogs.

Parts of human skeletons littered the shoreline of the Ganges River. Skulls stared at us while we rested on a grassy knoll overlooking the river.

Walking along the shore, I collected several rust-gold marigold flowers. As a symbolic gesture, I tossed them into the Holy River. Rather than float into eternity, most stuck in the mud a short distance from shore. The river was not attractive. Bits of floating charcoal meandered in the sluggish brown current. Muddied white burial shrouds and a lone purple sari wavered in the current. Young children, three to eight years of age, barely glanced at the burning pyres. They were busy collecting dung from a group of wandering water buffalo. This dung would fuel the next cremation.

The government tried several creative approaches to clean up the river. One solution was to breed and release crocodiles and flesh-eating turtles into the Ganges. Over 40,000 turtles were released into the river of death. The turtles' and crocodiles' job was to eat partially burned bodies that were cast into the river. But in a land where food is scarce, the turtles and crocodiles, which were to eat the dead, were eaten by the living.

As I watched the riverside burning of deceased relatives, I thought about the efficiency of our own cremations. Our industrialized handling of the dead creates a consistent powder-flake product compared to the bits and pieces left over from a Ganges pyre, but our sterilized ritual has no participation from family members when compared to the crowds of relatives surrounding the funeral pyres on the banks of the Ganges. The size of Indian families makes death commonplace. Rajveer, one Indian man I spoke with, said, "I have eighty relatives that I know well. I'm thirty-five and have been to fifteen funerals in my lifetime."

As I watched the river, Dan walked up to me.

"Could you watch the camels for a while?" asked Dan.

"Sure," I said. "What are you up to?"

"I want to collect some Ganges water," he said.

"Why?"

"The Ganges is a sacred river for Hindus," explained Dan. "People all over Asia believe it has healing power. I want to collect some for a family I know in Nepal. A gift of Ganges water is really appreciated. There are dishonest people who fill water bottles out of their tap and label it Ganges water. Then they sell it to the faithful. People never know if they are getting the real thing, so when a trusted friend brings it, they know it is genuine."

That was Dan, always thinking about other people and what he could do for them.

He collected the water in two empty Pepsi bottles. The water was as brown as the bottles' original contents. After seeing all the "stuff" floating in the water, I thought, *It may not heal people, but if they survived drinking the foul-looking liquid it could only make them stronger.*

Dan collects two bottles of Ganges water to give to friends in Nepal.

Sam Goes to One Peg

"Oh, geez," I said in frustration. "Sam stepped on her reins again. I've gotten another broken nose peg."

Blood dripped from her nostril as I inspected it.

"That's the third time this week," I said while stroking her head. "The way she's been shaking her head lately tells me she's hurting. I've been using that antibiotic spray but it doesn't seem to be helping."

"I don't think her nose is going to heal if we leave the peg in," observed Dan. "The wound rubs against the peg. Can you control her with just one peg?"

"If I'm walking, yes," I said. "But I'm not going to ride her with a single peg. That would be pushing my luck."

"Whot' do you want to do?"

I looked at Sam who stared back at me miserably. "I guess we take out the peg and I walk the rest of the way."

Dan and I were no longer nose peg amateurs. After tying Sam's front legs together so she couldn't kick us, I grabbed Sam's lower lip and held her head steady while Dan wove a big, thick bamboo stick into her halter. Sam knew what was coming and expressed her displeasure by regurgitating on my arm. Wiping the slime off, I lowered her head to the ground, and Dan and I stood on the stick. Our combined weight on the stick barely kept her from wildly swinging her head about and knocking us around like cue balls. Dr. Dan, now an expert at sticking his fingers up camel noses, ignored Sam's roars and bared teeth as he removed the peg.

"What about Raika?" I asked, pointing in her direction. Raika had spent the last two weeks testing her titanium nose by yanking against her reins. Getting jerked around could put Dan into a foul mood. One time, when she was tethered to a tree, she pulled back against her reins so hard he thought the reins would snap. All this abuse had finally caused an infection in one nostril.

"I'd have to be daft to take out one of her pegs," said Dan. "She's hard enough to control with two. She's pushed me into traffic and tried to get herself killed by running in front of buses and trucks. I'd rather wrap a turban on a wild pig than try to control her with one peg." Of course Dan was right. Controlling Raika with one peg could get Raika or Dan killed when she went out of control on the roadway.

A decision was made that we would both walk from now on. It was day 87.

Nepal?

Time was running out. My return flight to the U.S. was set so that I would be home in time for my son's birthday. We only had a week left. Our final big goal would be to make it to the Western border of Nepal near the town of Tanakpur, but this meant we needed to cover over thirty miles per day. We had hit a lot of eighteen to twenty mile days, but that was our best.

To make it to Nepal would be a first for two foreigners on camels. But it was a long shot. We had come a good distance and had many amazing experiences already. At night we talked back and forth between our tents trying to figure out a way we could make it.

"I think we have a chance of getting to Nepal," I said. "We get up at first light and walk till nightfall. Plus we only take time for one meal a day. You wanted to lose more weight, didn't you?"

"You mean more than the forty pounds I've already left on the trail? I don't think just walking more each day is going to add enough mileage."

"I agree. We need to hitch more rides on fast carts and tow the camels behind. I've checked the maps. We might pull it off."

Dan thought about it and then said, "I'm up for a bit of a challenge. Set your watch for 6:00 A.M. See you in the morning."

Thus began our marathon race towards the Nepal border. One of our biggest problems was food. Weeks before we had gotten rid of our stoves, fuel bottles, and pots and pans. Cooking gear took up too much space, and it took too much time to cook. We had switched over to fast food. Not MacDonald's or Taco Bell. Our fast food consisted of bread or chapatti, tomatoes purified in chlorinated water, onions, and canned cheese. Sometimes we bought hard-boiled eggs, but only if they were still in the shell. If they were already peeled it was a health risk. We loved potato pancakes bought hot from vendors along the road. Bananas were a staple. We bought forty to fifty pounds of bananas at a time for the camels and sneaked a couple for our own meals. We also had what Dan called potatoes-in-a-bag, potato chips. I satisfied my craving for protein by carrying bags of peanuts. Sam quickly learned to hang her head over my shoulder where she could slurp up a peanut before it made it to my mouth.

Sometimes we feasted. A banquet included canned beans, 7-Up, and orange cookies. The great explorer, Admiral Byrd, said, "Half the problems in the world come from not knowing how little we need." Dan and I discovered just how little we needed to be content.

Our meals were simple even when we had access to more elaborate Indian cuisine. My problem with the local food was that my mouth was not lined with asbestos. Take *samosas* for instance. Samosas made me think of my brother-in-law, Tom. Tom loves spoonfuls of Tabasco, dragon's breath hot chili, and Mad Dog Magma Sauce, anything that, as he says, "Ignites the taste buds." Biting into the puffed pastry shell of a zesty samosa is as pleasurable as pouring gasoline down your throat and tossing in a match. Even Dan had problems with the spiciness of the food we found on the road, and he is willing to eat almost anything, including the British delicacy Marmite, which looks and tastes like tractor grease. Actually, tractor grease tastes better.

Dan, the camels, and I all lost weight. I dropped thirty pounds from the beginning of the trip. Nevertheless, we didn't skimp on the camels. People told us we would not find food for them this far from the desert. But we discovered that Sam was a banana addict. She sucked up twenty pounds of bananas, peel included, faster than a shop vacuum. Sometimes I counted my fingers after feeding her. Raika wasn't as banana crazy, but both Raika and Sam were fond of peanuts. They could eat seven pounds at a meal, shells and all. Before going to bed at night, Dan and I climbed into neem trees and cut down branches for camel midnight snacks. We also discovered that our camels had a sweet tooth. They loved sugar cane, and we were now surrounded by fields of the stuff.

In the mornings we woke early in heavy mist, a big change from months ago in the desert. We packed our damp tents and gear. At night we slept in clammy blankets rather than take time to dry them during the day.

We also became experts at hiring carts: donkey carts, horse carts, or oxen carts. We sat on the back of a jostling two-wheeled wagon, lying against our gear as the girls trotted behind to keep up. When a cart ride was over and we were back on foot, we set a furious pace. As the sun neared the horizon, Dan or I would nudge the other to start jogging. We wanted to squeeze in one more mile before the sun set. We pushed our distance to thirty miles a day. There was also another good reason for moving fast.

Bandits

Indian friends, police, and military officials warned us about the area between Agra and Nepal. They all cautioned us to "Watch out for bandits." There was one problem with this advice. No one told us what a bandit looked like. We saw men on motorcycles with shotguns cruising the road. We weren't sure if they were good guys or bad guys. We cautiously approached one armed rider and asked, "Why the shotgun?" He simply replied, "Security."

The police told us, "Make sure you are off the road by 5:00 P.M. And make sure that no one sees where you camp." So we picked concealed campsites behind hay bales, hidden by trees, or screened by tall sugar-cane plants. When there were no good hiding places to camp, we relied on the change in climate to hide us. We simply walked into the evening mist far enough from the road where no one would spot us.

Good guys or bad guys with a shotgun? We were never sure.

It wasn't only the climate that changed during the course of our trip. The landscape had also morphed. The desert was replaced with lush green fields. Sometimes the road we followed ran through a tunnel of trees, mile after mile of shade. Water was everywhere. There was so much water that rice was now the preferred crop, growing in submerged fields. Surprisingly, we saw hardly any mosquitoes. But rather than be lured into complacency by this seeming lack of mosquitoes, we slept in our tents religiously. I wore my mosquito Buzz Off clothing during the day and slept in it at night. It was impregnated with a chemical to keep bloodsuckers from biting through the cloth. I lit a mosquito coil inside my tent every night before bed. I wanted to make sure I didn't share my tent with any malaria-carrying bugs.

Big Danger, Tiny Package

Globetrotting adventurers learn that the biggest dangers they face are from the smallest critters. Every year over one million people die from malaria. It is the leading cause of disease and death worldwide. Malaria is a parasite that is transmitted to humans by the bite of a female Anopheles mosquito. Some strains of malaria are particularly dangerous. *Plasmodium falciparum* (one of four malarial parasites) can cause death within twelve to forty-eight hours after the appearance of symptoms. This is why insect repellants, mosquito resistant clothing, mosquito nets, and preventive drugs are some of the precautions used by travelers. The last one, preventive drugs, is not a guarantee of safety. Drugs can also have side effects. They can lead to dizziness, vision problems, hair falling out, vomiting—it's one reason that some explorers avoid the drugs and rely on the other precautions.

At this point on the expedition we had passed more religious temples and shrines than there are McDonald's in the world. At the beginning of our trip, in the state of Rajasthan, we saw ancient structures and simple statuary. In the state of Uttar Pradesh, the religious symbols took on a modern appearance. Rather than work in traditional stone, the religious artisans of the area introduced fiberglass and colored resins. The many-armed god Shiva, and the monkey god, Hanuman, were represented by glistening fiberglass statues.

The monkey god, Hanuman.

The people were also different. Part of the change was in their clothing. In the desert, the women wore eye-catching peacock blues, robin reds, and gold-embroidered saris. Now, farther north, they dressed in dull sparrow browns and rust colors. The muted colors matched their personalities. Adults were subdued. People still looked at us, but they no longer hung around watching us till nightfall. Privacy was back in fashion.

In the early part of our trip, when we approached a village there would be cries from the children, *gora-gora* (foreigner, foreigner), followed by *untnee-untnee* (camel, camel). Now we heard *untnee-untnee* followed by *gora-gora*. Our camels were now more novel than we were. At one stop, a man stuck a pan under Raika as she urinated. Camel urine is believed to be good medicine, but it is hard to obtain this far from the desert, so even our camels' pee was special. This novelty affected both people and livestock.

In the desert state of Rajasthan where there are lots of camels, a water buffalo glanced at a camel with jaded disinterest. In the state of Uttar Pradesh where camels are rare, water buffalos broke chains and ripped wooden posts from the ground in their frenzy to escape from Sam and Raika. Many times we unintentionally stampeded animals. All we could do was yell an apology to the back of a chasing, cursing herder. This camel naiveté on the part of locals meant we no longer had to deal with advice on how to pack, saddle, ride, feed, tie, or treat our dromedaries. This lack of advice was a welcome change. We had more important things to concentrate on.

In order to increase our daily mileage we had to hitch rides. We soon learned that riding on an ox-cart was slower than walking. So, unless we were bone tired, we passed on ox-cart rides. Our favorite hitched rides were on horse carts, tongas. Horse carts were fast. Whenever we saw an approaching tonga we flagged it down. Dan or I would haggle with the driver over the price for a ride to the next town. Then we loaded our gear in the tonga and towed the camels. Often we carried five or six pounds of bananas in the tonga. That way we could treat our camels as they loped along behind the cart. There was a problem with this arrangement. When a big overcrowded bus or lorry came up behind the cart, the camels freaked out. Sam and Raika broke into a full run and tried to outrace the tonga. This required that Dan or I leap off a racing cart to keep control of the camels. It was never boring.

To keep up my energy for these surprise camel sprints, I depended on *chai* (tea). At the beginning of our trip, our good friend Katea-ram proved that you could walk many miles with no more sustenance than a glass of tea. Indian chai is nothing like its watery Western cousin. To compare the two would be like comparing a pencil-necked geek to a pumped weight lifter. Chai is made with black tea, buffalo milk, ginger root, and lots of sugar. It is rural India's version of a high-energy Jamba Juice smoothie. It provides liquid, protein, carbohydrates, and some vitamins. Whenever I spotted a chai seller, I stopped and filled up. "Two liters, please."

A roadside *chai* (tea) seller. Would you buy tea from this man?

Choosing a chai seller is an art—if you care about hygiene. I checked three things: location, seller, and process. First, I noted the stall's location. If it was over a fly infested sewer, common in towns, I kept walking. I preferred chai stands on a country road where there was less pollution and they were more likely to use fresh milk. Then there's the water used in the tea. I looked for a nearby well pump and checked that it was capped. If I saw the seller scooping water from an open well surrounded by water buffalo manure, it wasn't worth the risk. Next, I inspected the seller. The eyes can tell a lot. Yellow eyes may indicate hepatitis, smart to avoid. Mottling of the skin may be a sign of leprosy. Then the vendor's clothing, is it reasonably clean, or is he coughing up sputum and wiping it away with his sleeve? Last came process. Is the tea brought to a roiling boil two times? If the tea passed all my checks, I asked that the scalding liquid be poured directly into my own container. I was leery of the cups at roadside stands. They were often polished on the sleeves of vendors' shirts or with a rag that I wouldn't use to clean a toilet seat.

I'm still puzzled over the health standards. They are so different from Western standards. I saw hospitals that required you to hop over an open sewer to get to the entrance. One clinic's waiting room had outdoor beds that straddled an unwholesome muck. Each bed contained a patient. This violated everything I have been taught. You'd expect to see legions of ill. Yet, there didn't seem to be unreasonable signs of sickness. Maybe exposure makes for a tougher immune system.

Checkpoint

Checkpoints began to appear along the road, manned by police. Up to this point we simply waved and walked on. Not so near Pilibhit.

As we approached the barricade, an officer bathing under a hand water pump spied us. He stopped bathing, wrapped a towel around his waist, and approached us holding up his hand for us to stop. He looked pretty ridiculous.

"Whose camels are these?" he demanded in an official voice.

"They're ours," I replied.

Then he surprised me when he asked, "Where is your proof that these camels aren't stolen?"

He said this in such a way as to make it sound like foreigners routinely come to India to rustle camels in the Thar Desert and smuggle them across India.

"I think you have the bill of sale," said Dan.

I had to get Sam to kneel so that I could get at my duffle bag. I rummaged through my gear trying to find where I had stuffed our official papers. The ropes lashed across my duffle bag made it difficult to get my hand into the opening without completely untying the pack, a tedious process.

"It's in here someplace," I said. Then I came across a newspaper article written about our trip. "Will this do instead?" I handed the article to him.

He looked carefully at the photos in the article, comparing them with our own likenesses. Then he looked at the camels' photos to make sure they matched our group. Then he proceeded to read the whole article.

Dan whispered, "Get off, he probably thinks we faked the article with Photoshop so we could sneak camels past unsuspecting security guards."

I shushed Dan. I didn't want to end up in a local jail while they checked our ownership.

"A bill of sale is not necessary," said the officer as he dropped the towel and went back to bathing.

As we walked on, I said to Dan, "I wonder how I would feel if a highway patrol officer in the U.S. pulled me over and got out of his car in his underpants."

"More importantly," added Dan, "what would he have done if we were desperate camel thieves? Would he have threatened to snap us with his towel?"

Short Cut

We were now almost all the way through November. Not much time remained to make it to Nepal. Often we woke up surrounded by a heavy graveyard mist that hung around most of the day. While packing our wet gear, I said to Dan, "We should make a movie called *Camels in the Mist.*"

This far north, we often woke to a mist-shrouded sunrise.

To make our thirty-mile-a-day quota, we hired any cart that passed by. One day we rented a tonga with a small horse. It looked like the pony you see at a child's birthday party. When Dan and I sat on the back of the cart, our combined weight lifted the tiny pony off the ground. The driver tugged and pulled on us. He wanted to better balance the cart. Finally we got the right distribution of weight and headed down the road. Our pony was reluctant to go and the driver banged a brick on the cart. Sometimes this was enough to get the horse moving. When banging the cart didn't work, he banged the rump of the pony with the brick. Dan and I winced each time he used this technique.

Up to this point, our route finding had been, as Dan put it, "Spot on." We'd been quite accurate with our cheap road atlas. Now with no time for a mistake, we were confused. The press made every newspaper reader aware of who we were. When we walked down the road, people held up newspapers, pointing to articles about us, and yelled, "Nepal, Nepal," our destination. Our confusion stemmed from the advice we were given. Some people told us the border crossing to Nepal was on the road to Tanakpur. Others said there was a short cut. Our map supported the Tanakpur crossing. In our self-imposed deadline, we only had one day left. Which would it be? Short cut or Tanakpur? We chose the short cut. This decision was made because there was no way we were going to make it to Tanakpur within our deadline. Karma was on our side again.

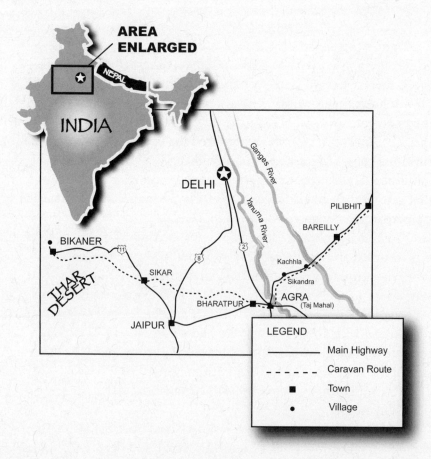

Border Crossing

The border crossing with Nepal is a short distance from a small
border town. It's on the other side of the cleanest river we saw in
India. Here again we faced a challenge. We shuffled along with the
flow of humanity towards a bridge, but when we got to the bridge,
the main gate was padlocked. The only way to get onto the span was
through a narrow turnstile. I measured the opening. It was too narrow for a camel. We asked a guard with a gun to open the gate. He
motioned us through. Using sign language and Hindi, I explained
that getting the camels through the turnstile would be like trying to
squeeze a camel through the eye of a needle.

"You have problem?" asked a scruffy looking man. His clothing
was rumpled and his breath was 90-proof alcohol. We weren't sure
if he was simply a drunk or an official drunk. He motioned us to
stay where we were while he weaved off in the opposite direction.
We stood looking at the guard with the gun. In moments our drunk
reappeared with another man who had a ring of keys. He opened
the gate for our dromedaries and waved us through. On the other
side of the river was the Indian immigration office.

"I'm not going to cross over into Nepal," said Dan.

"Why not?"

"My visa's only good for one visit to Nepal this year. After the
camel trip I'm going to visit friends in Nepal, so I don't want to use
up my visa. If one of us makes it, that's good enough. Think of it
like a climb on Mt. Everest. Not everyone on the team makes it to

the top. The important thing is that some of the climbers make it. You go for it. Cheers."

While Dan went down to the beach and made himself comfortable, I entered immigration.

A border official waved for me to sit down. Our conversation was carried on in broken Hindi and English.

"I would like to cross into Nepal today and return back to India today as well," I said.

The official looked thoughtful, "You wish to come back today?"

"Yes, I already have a Nepalese visa."

"That is not possible," said the official shaking his head. "It will take at least one week to prepare the necessary paperwork for you to return to India."

"I'm sorry. I don't understand. I have my passport in order and was told that crossing the border was a simple process of your checking my papers."

The official looked at me for a moment, took my passport, and paged through it. He looked at me expectantly. I felt kind of stupid, like I wasn't getting something. Then he handed back my passport and said, "It is not possible."

While I stewed over this, a bored looking individual and two nervous Nepalese were escorted into the room by an armed guard. My concerns took back seat as a mini-drama unfolded before me. The border official spoke in an angry tone of voice to the three individuals. The bored individual only said a few words in a calm tone. This seemed to make the border official furious and he started yelling. He seemed so angry I thought he'd ask the armed guard to shoot someone just to let off steam. I was paying close attention, so I clearly saw the bored individual slip a wad of bills into the immigration official's hand. It was a smooth move. It had the look of being much practiced. The immigration official immediately ended his tantrum and waved the offending trio through the border. I had just witnessed an experienced border-crosser pass a bribe.

The official turned back to me. He looked at me knowingly, then said, "I might be able to get the necessary paperwork ready if you would leave a deposit."

"How much would this deposit be?" I asked.

"Let's say two hundred rupees?"

I paid the "deposit" and was given the necessary stamps to exit India. "Oh," said the official, "You must be back by 6:00 P.M., after which we close."

I had less than two hours to get to Nepal. I still had to go through another checkpoint where the crossing guards said in Hindi, "Camel? *No* camel." I could go through but not the camel.

"To bring a camel from India," said the guard in Hindi, "you need proper authorization."

My guess was that this was the first time anyone had ever tried to bring a camel across this particular border crossing. I bluffed and said, "I just came from immigration and they gave me authorization." Then I acted like I didn't understand a word he said. I just kept showing him my passport and stamps. He finally gave up and passed both of us through. At least there was one bribe I wouldn't have to pay.

Walking about a mile through the separation area between India and Nepal, I came to the Nepalese immigration office. An elderly man was in charge. Through an interpreter he asked, "You only want to cross the border, then return?" He looked confused. The presence of a camel in my luggage added to his bewilderment.

"That is your camel?"

"Yes."

"Where did you get a camel?" The tone of his voice suggested that seeing a camel this far North was very unusual.

"In Bikaner near the Pakistan border."

"But how did you get the camel here?"

"I rode it."

He shook his head as if this information was too hard to process. Finally, he focused on something he understood. He looked at the Nepalese visa in my passport. "Your visa is only good for six months."

"Yes," I replied, and then to be helpful, "It was stamped June 16, which means it is good until December 16. I have several more weeks."

He had difficulty with the math. "Visa is expired," he said.

I tried taking him through the math, but my Hindi was not up to the task, nor were his arithmetic skills. It was only when a young assistant stepped in to help that the math got straightened out. Not only did I get my entry visa stamped, but my exit visa as well. Probably the fastest Nepal turn-around visit on record. They requested that I take a picture of them standing next to my camel with assurances that I would send them a copy.

Even with all this official stamping, I still had to make my way to the actual gate that would take me into Nepal. At that gate there was another official. The lenses on his glasses were as thick as Coke bottles. He said, "You need to go to immigration for the proper paperwork."

"I just came from there," I said pointing at the building fifty feet behind me. "See the stamps in my passport? Here's the visa."

He ignored me, "You must go to immigration."

"Look, use that phone on the wall, and they will tell you I just came from there."

"No, you must go to immigration."

We went back and forth. I was tempted to pluck off his glasses, which probably would have left him blind, and then run past him. That's when Sam helped out. She poked her head into the door of the guardhouse where the gatekeeper sat. I didn't scold her. I'm sure this was the first time the gatekeeper had come nose to nose with a camel. Sam opened her mouth and he got a good look at her teeth. He grabbed the phone on the wall behind him and called for back up, all the time staring at Sam. The youthful assistant who had helped me earlier jogged the short distance from immigration. He cleared things up. Finally the gate was lifted. Sam and I officially crossed into Nepal.

On the Nepalese side I did a victory dance to the amusement of the locals. Everyone wanted their pictures taken with Sam. Sam wasn't pleased with the attention. She was experiencing separation anxiety from Raika. Camels are social animals, and even though the Sam-Raika relationship was a rocky one, any camel company was better than no camel company.

Our expedition had made it! Then I calmed down and remembered a story every seasoned mountain climber has heard. Upon reaching the top of a difficult peak a novice climber exclaimed to his partner, "We made it!" To which the experienced climber replied, "No. We've made it half-way. We still need to get back down." The trip wasn't over yet. It was day 91.

While taking photographs, I was reminded, as I had been by the border official, that there were serious problems with Maoist rebels in Nepal. A pickup truck cruised by filled with blue-uniformed military personnel with their weapons at the ready. They swept through the area pausing to look at Sam.

Then it was time for me to jog back to the Indian side of the border. We made it just before immigration closed. The entry paperwork paid for with my "deposit" was waiting.

I asked the official, "It's getting dark. Can we cross back over the bridge tomorrow? It would be easier on us if we could stay on the riverbank on this side tonight." He surprised me by saying, "Yes." No "deposit" was necessary.

This freebie may be partly due to Dan. He had struck up a conversation with the official in my absence and did his usual friend-making magic.

Death Shrine

Dan and I walked a half-mile down the Kali River. It had been a long day. All we could think about was sleep. Neither of us had the energy to eat. In the dark I kicked some white sticks out of the way as I set up my tent. It was one of the best campsites of the trip. Our tents sat on a grassy knoll overlooking the river. There were several trees to tie Sam and Raika to. Nothing disturbed our sleep except for the sound of thunder. A storm might be brewing, but we had our rainflys over the tents. Dan and I slipped into exhausted sleep.

In the morning I was surprised to see that the "white sticks" I had carelessly kicked about the previous evening were human bones. The source of the bones was the nearby riverbank. It was littered with the unburnt remains of funeral pyres. There was also another macabre feature I had missed in the darkness. A feature that, had we seen it, would have certainly spooked us into looking for another campsite. A tree near my tent was swathed in a tattered blood red cloth. At the base of the tree sat three human skulls, one child and two adults. The skulls were carefully laid out and ringed by an odd assortment of items: razor blades, coins, femurs, ribs, pictures of gods, and a trident.

A death shrine next to our campsite on the border of India and Nepal.

Dan and I started packing. Out of the corner of my eye I saw a scarecrow thin man approach the tree. In his arms were items that had escaped the flames of a funeral pyre. Overcome by curiosity, Dan fished something out of his camel pack and nodded at me to follow. Dan approached the scarecrow man and said, *Namaste*, and held out a cigar. The man accepted the gift and motioned for us to sit down. In broken Hindi and Nepali (Dan speaks Nepali), we learned that both Indians and Nepalese bring their dead to this section of the river. He pointed at the river. Judging from the many bits of bones I saw along the shore, I imagined the bottom of the river littered with skeletons. The Kali River is a substitute holy river. The faithful don't have to travel all the way to the Ganges to burn their dead. Eventually the Kali flows into the Ganges. As we talked, the man spread some soaked grain on a mat in the sun to dry. It had been spilled on the ground next to one of the funeral pyres. He told us he was a caretaker for the dead. The drying grain was to be his next meal.

Interrogation

We finished packing and left the gaunt man smoking his cigar. Not far up the river, we passed a military base. The guards motioned us over. "Passports and visa please," said the guard. He looked at us suspiciously.

We were told to tie up our camels and escorted inside a barbwire-enclosed compound surrounded by manned sentry posts. Chairs and a table were brought outside and we were asked to sit down.

"Would you like tea or coffee?" asked our military escort.

"Tea, please."

"Cookies?"

"Yes."

The interrogation was off to a good start. A three-star general arrived and started asking questions.

"Do you know you are in a restricted area along the international border?"

"We asked for permission from the border officials last night who said it would be OK for us to camp here," I replied. Actually, we were somewhat loose in our interpretation of where we could camp. We had traveled about a half-mile down the river to get a little privacy. But who was measuring?

"Do you realize," asked the general, "that last night, a short distance from your camp, we engaged Maoist rebels in an ambush? Did you hear the explosions?"

Now that was a surprise. "Explosions?" I asked. "We thought it was thunder."

"No, no. We caught smugglers trying to bring weapons across the border," said the general. "You are lucky you weren't confused for rebels. You could have been shot."

Dan optimistically said, "The gods watch over us."

While Dan went to make a telephone call with the general, I sat there puzzled. How, I wondered, could two camels, standing over eight feet high and being led by two foreigners, sneak past this fortified encampment without anyone noticing or challenging us the night before?

I got up to walk around and stepped inside a sentry post to talk to the guard. "No pictures," he said, after I had snapped two shots. A diagram of the area he was supposed to watch was mounted on the sandbags. I looked through the rifle port and clearly saw where we had camped the night before. There was no way an alert sentry could miss us. I suspected that the police and military "interrogated" us just because we were a novelty and they were curious.

Later the general told us, "Problems with the Maoists and a lack of jobs force many Nepalese to seek work in India. One thousand to fifteen hundred Nepalese cross this border daily. Their honesty and hard-work ethic make them valued workers in India. After five or six months they return home with their earnings. But the border is also a site for drug and gun-running."

Again I was baffled. With an open border between India and Nepal that is over 900 miles long, you'd think smugglers would choose a spot further from police and military installations to sneak illegal stuff across.

The general wished us good luck on the rest of our journey.

We crossed back over the bridge into India and headed towards a small border town that didn't exist. At least it didn't exist on our map, nor did the road that led to it. While I tended the camels in the forest just outside this no-name town, Dan went looking for a truck. Our plan was to transport the girls back to Bikaner where we had originally started.

Waiting for Dan to return, I was joined by a group of three boys. They shyly glanced at the camels and scampered off into the forest. I watched from a distance as they unhooked ropes from their waists. The ropes had a stone attached to a loop in the end. Ignoring me, they whipped the rock-weighted ropes around their heads, tossing one end of the rope high into a tree. It looked like

a gaucho throwing a bolo. I had no idea what they were doing.
Occasionally one of the boys would scamper up the trunk of a tree.
I needed a closer look. Grabbing a handful of candy from my pack,
I approached them. Any reluctance they had in talking to me was
overcome by the candy.

The boys scampered up the trees like monkeys.

"What are you doing?" I asked in Hindi.
"Throw ropes into tree," explained their leader.
"Yes," I said. "But, why?"
"Small tree," he added helpfully.
"Small tree?" This wasn't making any sense.
I asked him to show me up close what he was doing. He
whipped the rope around his head and launched it into the air. It
wrapped around an upper branch as accurately as Indiana Jones
wrapping his whip around a villain. It was obvious he had done this
many times. Then he put all his weight on the dangling rope and

the branch gave a loud crack and came crashing down to the forest floor.

"See," he said, "Small tree," as if the explanation was obvious.

He read the look of confusion on my face and nodded to his buddies who picked up some of the wood and dropped it into a pile. Then he mimed lighting a match.

Then it hit me like the answer in a game of Charades, "You're collecting firewood." I rubbed my hands in front of the fake blaze.

"Yes," he nodded.

When they left the clearing they lugged armloads of "small trees."

The firewood cowboys are loaded up and headed home.

Truckophobia

Dan found some helpful police who, for a sum, came up with a truck driver who'd transport our camels to Jaipur. Jaipur was in the direction of Bikaner so we said yes. It was getting dark and we had to be loaded before nightfall to leave.

The truck was huge. Its thirty-foot long bed was designed to carry bags of concrete. Grey powder from a recent load coated the bed. Here's where things got interesting. The bed of the truck was five feet off the ground. The driver backed up to a convenient dirt ramp, but the bed was still three feet from the ground. We'd seen the camels jump over higher obstacles, but Raika had truckophobia. We tried luring, dragging, and pushing her onto the truck, but an animal that can pull a cart with a 2,000-pound load is going to win any tug-of-war with puny humans. Even with five people pulling a rope around her neck, she wouldn't budge. Twice in the struggle, I was almost strangled by the rope when she whipped around.

Afraid of losing our ride, I asked some onlookers, "Does anyone know of another ramp in town?"

"Yes," said an old man. "There is a ramp near the train station."

"Can you take me there?" I asked.

"Yes, of course," he replied.

I followed him to the train station and a concrete loading dock. I measured the height. It was perfect. Another measurement wasn't so perfect. The distance from the ramp to a concrete wall was forty-one feet. Our truck was thirty-nine feet long. The driver would have only two feet to maneuver his monster truck. In an impressive backing display, the driver got the truck into the tight space. But Raika had had it with trucks. This is when we had a near camel calamity. She walked onto the ramp. Then she saw the truck. Her body language said, "In your dreams." While trying to pull her the rest of the way up the ramp and onto the truck bed, she violently yanked us around. To escape the truck she plunged off the platform, a height of about five feet. Her back legs buckled as she slid over the edge, but she managed to land on her front legs, narrowly avoiding a bone-crushing fall.

That was it for Dan.

"It's turkey time," hissed Dan. "Get her as close to the truck as you can."

Pretending not to notice the truck I got her within ten feet. "How's that?" I asked.

"That's the best we're going to do," said Dan.

I made the breathy *Jai* sound signaling Raika to kneel. Dan brandished his bamboo cane to reinforce my command.

"Help me hobble her," instructed Dan.

He tied both her front and back legs together, making it impossible for her to rise.

By now, we had attracted a crowd. Part of the group consisted of Indian soldiers, a Gurka regiment. One spoke English and Dan struck up a conversation.

"You blokes strong enough to lift a camel?" asked Dan.

The soldiers saw it as great fun. While they weren't able to lift Raika, we did manage to shove her onto the truck like an oversized hockey puck.

Sam, who had not been frightened by the initial truck loading attempts, simply walked onto the truck bed. She obediently kneeled and we tied her up. Sam's initial calmness disappeared when the truck started moving. Even though she was secured with wide banded trusses, she snapped the one on her haunches and threatened to back over the low tailgate. I dove for her neck, while Dan tackled her rising rump. There was no way for us to signal the driver to stop. Desperately holding Sam down on the moving truck, Dan risked reaching under her body to retie her. I clung to her head trying to prevent her from lifting me into the air. Over and over I repeated, "calm, calm, calm," words I used whenever she was stressed. As I repeated the soothing phrase, I imagined what would happen to a camel that tumbled out of a truck going 30 mph. It was close, but we quieted her down and retied the ropes.

Later the driver invited us to ride in the cab. We turned down his offer and told him we needed to stay next to the camels or they would freak out. We shared the truck bed with six other Indian hitchhikers. They were better prepared for what I can only describe as a twenty-eight-hour body slam fest. The experienced hitchhikers had brought two-foot thick bundles of pads to shield them from the truck bed. Plus they had thick quilts to wrap up in when it got cold. Dan and I curled up in thin blankets on a thinner layer of straw we had spread over the truck bed. I snuggled in next to Sam who seemed to gain comfort from my presence, resting her head next to

me, or hovering just above my body. Every time we hit a pothole—
which was about every twenty feet—we levitated and then redis-
covered gravity, slamming back down onto the metal truck bed. I've
experienced fewer body blows in full-contact karate. In no time I
had a boxer's headache. After an hour my internal organs felt like
they had been whacked with a cricket bat. My kidneys threatened
to wet my pants with every impact.

The fine-powdered cement left over from the last shipment
coated everything. We got dirtier in the first ten minutes of this ride
than we had gotten in the previous ten weeks. The cement sucked
the moisture out of my skin and then began to harden. My face felt
like I was wearing a dried mud plaster.

Getting battered by the truck was only one of our problems.
Not far down the road, a policeman stopped us. He wasn't subtle
like the immigration official had been. He said, "*Baksheesh*. Give
me a thousand rupees and you can go on."

The driver shook his head sadly and replied, "You are taking the
bread out of my mouth." This repartee went back and forth with the
officer eventually settling on twenty rupees.

The second time we were stopped was in the early morning.
It was a police jeep out hunting trucks—a shark cruising for prey.
This shark was more serious than the previous barracuda. The jeep
held three police. They pulled us over.

"Your license plates are wrong," said one of the policemen to the
driver.

I had to admit they did look suspiciously grimy, like someone
had painted them with muck.

Then spotting the camels, the officer quickly said, "You are not
authorized to carry camels." Of course that was ridiculous, trucks in
India carry whatever they can.

The driver sensed the seriousness of the situation. He immediately offered a roll of rupees. The officer slapped the money away
and started yelling and cuffing the driver in the head with the back
of his hand. Our driver covered his head protectively and tried to
apologize for offering such a small amount but it was all he had.
Then the policeman reached for a bamboo cane held by another

officer. He was preparing to beat the driver. That's when Dan and I appeared, jumping off the back of the truck.

This surprised the officers. They had not noticed the dust covered turban-wearing adventurers among the other hitchhikers.

I approached the baton-wielding policeman and said, "The camels are ours. Is there a problem?"

He grabbed my arm. I pulled away and gave him a steely Clint Eastwood stare. I don't think he was prepared for the Clint Squint. Like a shark, he was used to his prey cowering.

Sensing more rupees than the truck driver could afford, the policeman said, "They your camels. Then where receipt?"

While Dan searched for the receipt, I explained Dan's beloved, almost Walter Cronkite-like status with the BBC, flaunted my journalist credentials (I had my National Geographic Society membership card which looks official when glanced at), and mentioned all the mayors and district magistrates we had met along our route.

Taking the camel seller's receipt from Dan, and looking at it disdainfully, he said, "Receipt for camels is invalid."

"Why?" I countered. "It's written in Hindi and English. It has the sellers' signatures and witnesses."

He sneered, "It doesn't have official seal."

"What would be an official seal?" I insisted.

He just repeated, "No official seal. Give me 3,000 rupees and we can fix the problem."

At this point, Dan became very obliging, "We'd be glad to give you the money."

I looked at Dan like he was a moron. We didn't have 3,000 rupees to squander on a bribe. Not to mention, every policeman from here to Jaipur would be on the lookout for the generous foreigners.

But Dan was more clever than that. He continued, "The powerful international charity we work for requires a receipt."

Now I got his drift. I promptly started writing a receipt and taking down the names of the officers. I also said, "We can use our phone to call some of the important people we know in the area to make sure it is done right."

The policeman sniggered, "Cell phones don't work here." It was obvious they were experts at picking a good place to rip off truck drivers.

"That's not a problem," I replied confidently. "You see this? It is an Iridium satellite phone." I took the phone out of its case and raised the antenna. "It works anyplace."

When I moved towards the jeep to take down the license plate number, an older officer standing nearby moved in front of the license plate and said something in clipped Hindi. He was obviously in charge. The two junior officers responded like underlings respectful of a mob boss. What he said caused an immediate turnaround.

The policeman standing near me thrust his hand towards me. It was such a quick movement that I almost instinctively slapped it away. Fortunately, I suppressed the motion. The policeman was reaching to shake my hand. "Please continue on your way," he smiled, "We wish you a good stay in India." With that they leaped into the jeep and were gone in a swirl of dust. It wasn't our last encounter with rupee-hungry police, but we had gotten through the worst of it.

Dan and our two girls in the back of a truck headed to Jaipur.

Jaipur

After twenty-eight hours of banging around in the back of the truck, we arrived in Jaipur, the city of pink forts, an island palace, and elephants. Of course we saw none of the city's grandeur. It was late at night. This was as far as the truck would take us. In the dark, we drove around looking for a good place to unload camels.

"Look over there," I said banging on the back of the truck to get the driver's attention. "That pile of sand might work."

Our driver backed up to the makeshift unloading dock. Dan and I jumped down and started pushing the sand up to the back edge of the truck bed. We tried to create a ramp.

Sam came off easily. Raika, true to her nature, made things difficult. Her behavior reminded me of my eight-year-old son's attitude towards bathing. When I try to get Griffin to take a bath, he comes up with every excuse for avoiding it. Once he's in the water, it takes a shark in the tub to get him out. In a similar manner, Raika battled us when we tried to load her and now she didn't want to come off the truck.

"I say we set the truck on fire," suggested Dan. "That might get her to move."

Fortunately, we didn't have to burn the truck. When we tried to turn Raika around to face the tailgate, she balked and started pulling backwards, eventually stumbling off the truck rear first and almost falling on top of me.

We paid the driver and added an extra big wad of rupees. He had helped us drag the camels on and off the truck, gotten slapped around by the police, and driven for twenty-eight hours without sleep to get us to Jaipur. Like many Indians who deal with hardship in their lives, he smiled happily as he took the money and wished us a good journey.

Making it to Jaipur was a relief. Our friend, Ranveer Singh, the man who had donated our riding saddles, had relatives in Jaipur. He made arrangements for us to stay in one of his beautiful homes on the outskirts of town. We parked our camels in a back yard that was occupied by a cow and a water buffalo. When I asked why a mansion would have a courtyard for a cow and a water buffalo, I

was told that having your own source of fresh milk is still valued—
even among the rich.

During the layover, we called a local veterinarian. We asked if
he would make a house call. Raika needed a checkup. During the
last few days of the trip, she had started shaking her head as if trying to rid herself of a pesky fly. A quick inspection showed that her
problem was fly related. She had maggots growing inside her nostrils. The same problem that had plagued Humper and GB. All the
months of stubbornly tugging and yanking on her reins had finally
damaged her titanium nose.

We knew she was sick. She no longer acted like a pampered tantrum queen. When the veterinarian asked us to hold her head, she
struggled feebly as he swabbed her nose with kerosene to kill the fly
larvae. The vet assured us she would be fine after a few days of rest.
We left her to rest with a pile of traditional desert camel food.

Camel Talk VII

"Food. Proper food," groaned Raika as she nibbled at the straw pile
in front of her. "Finally, something dry. Something that has to be
chewed. If I never see one of those mushy yellow fruits again, it will
be too soon. But I'm so tired."

"Riding in the giant dung beetle was hard," said Sam. Even
with all the pain that Raika had inflicted, Sam responded
sympathetically.

"I feel like a herd of water buffalos has run across my bones."

"It will get better," said Sam.

"What do you know?" countered Raika.

"Look," replied Sam, "the cow and water buffalo don't run from
us."

Raika looked uninterestedly at the cow and water buffalo standing in the courtyard. They returned her look with equal disinterest.

"I know your nose must feel as if fire ants have made a nest
inside," said Sam, remembering her own nose problems—most
caused by Raika—"but if you could smell, you would know these

are desert dwellers, like us. Our camel scent does not frighten them." Sam paused. "I can smell sand."

"You can," said Raika hopefully.

"As Humper would have said, 'Dry, dry sand is our land,'" mimicked Sam. "I think we are going home."

Goodbye

During our short stay in Jaipur, we met twelve-year-old Lee-Ram. Lee was fascinated by the camels and wanted to help us when we went to tend them. Even though Lee had been born in a village in the desert, he knew little about camels. That was because he had left his family and village at ten years of age to go to work in the city. Lee was the family's houseboy. He made sure we had tea and meals, helped with our laundry, cleaned rooms, and ran errands. His workday went from sunup to sundown, seven days a week. His salary was 900 rupees a month ($18 U.S.). He didn't attend school. Every time we saw him, there was a big smile on his face. The smile wasn't because he didn't have to go to school. It was because many poor Indians don't have steady meals or any assurance for their futures. In Lee's village another year of drought meant his family would suffer great hardships just to survive. At least Lee had some stability. He had regular meals, a roof over his head, clothing, a wage—this was much better than wondering if he would eat tomorrow. Plus, he could send his wages to help his family back in the desert. I saw many Indian children working: youngsters sewing book spines together, kids weaving carpets, children weeding in the fields, a twelve-year-old mechanic rebuilding a jeep. These children are resourceful and appreciate any small thing that helps them survive.

The next morning was my last day in Jaipur. I got up early to say goodbye to Sam and Raika. Then Dan accompanied me to the bus station. I was headed back to Delhi to keep my promise to my son to be home in time for his birthday. Dan would stay in Jaipur for a few more days.

"Dan, I guess this is it," I said. "Time to say goodbye."

"Only temporarily," said Dan, a big smile on his face. "You'll see.

We'll do other adventures together. It's in our blood. It's just a matter of time."

"You know, there's one goal I didn't write in my list of 100 goals for the expedition. It may be the most significant thing we did."

"Whot's that?" asked Dan.

"An expedition is like water," I said. "It can either dissolve a friendship like washing away sand, or mixed with cement, it can strengthen the bond." I paused. "I think we got on tremendously. We watched out for each other. We divided up tasks so that each of us did what we did best. I'm not going to forget riding with you under a desert moon, galloping down sand tracks, and there's no one I'd rather wrestle camels with." Dan and I exchanged bear hugs.

"See you buddy."

"Cheers, mate."

I got onto the bus.

As I watched through the bus window I had mixed feelings. Part of me was reluctant to leave. Some of that reluctance was because I felt guilty leaving Dan by himself with the camels for the last leg of the journey. The guilt was balanced by an equal sense of relief. I was no longer responsible for the camels. A camel man told me that owning a camel is like being guardian to a five-year-old child. You make sure they don't wander off or run into the street. You deal patiently with their cranky moods and appetites. You teach them. You are on guard against camelnappers. Sometimes you discipline them when they are naughty or nurse them when they are sick. Being a camel parent is nonstop work. My promise to be home for my son's ninth birthday was both a commitment to my son and a useful excuse. For me, this was the end of the caravan.

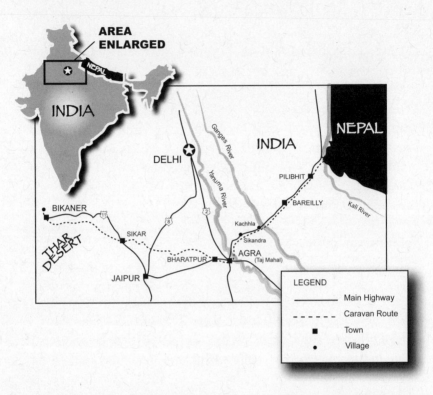

Our trip from Bikaner to Nepal took a number of months, yet the truck ride from Nepal back to Jaipur took little more than a day.

Epilogues

Epilogue 1

On the bus back to Delhi I sat next to an Indian gentleman. We struck up a conversation, and I learned that he was both a philosopher and an author. He asked what I was doing in India. As I talked with him about the expedition he became very interested in the solar lighting system Dan and I had installed. He then surprised me.

"You are a Buddhist," he said.

"No. Actually I don't know much about Buddhism."

"Actually you do. You don't have to label yourself a Buddhist to practice its wisdom. Your desire to do good in India, by the placement of your solar lights, is a sign of enlightenment. Buddhism teaches us that each person is like a page in a book. Just as each page is vital to the book, so is the book important to the individual. Doing good shows you recognize the importance of the book and not only your page in it."

"It was only a single light system."

"A wholesome action is a single deed. If each person contributes such a deed, it changes the nature of the story written in the book."

"I see."

"I have a question for you."

"Yes?"

"Does the earth have rights?"

"Rights?"

"Do we own the earth or does it have rights just like people do?"

"That's an unusual question."

"But an important one. You have seen a side of India that few Westerners see. Most Indians live a simple life. It's also a hard life. If we took the six billion people on the planet, many of whom live a hard life, and raised them to the standards of comfort you experience in America, how would it affect our planet?"

"It would be tough on the planet's resources."

"It would take five planet earths to have the resources necessary for such a change. So I pose a question, does the earth have rights? Is it part of the book we talked about?"

I never had a chance to answer his question. Just then the bus swerved. There was a loud *CACHUNKkkkk* sound as we sideswiped a flatbed truck carrying massive metal beams. Fortunately it was a glancing blow. The oversized truck could have easily pushed or flipped the bus off the road. The side of the bus was torn up, but after inspecting the damage, the driver decided to finish the trip. Again, karma was on my side.

I had a few days in Delhi to relax before the plane trip home. During that time I visited Mahatma Gandhi's memorial, attended a Bollywood movie (India's version of Hollywood produces more films than the U.S.), bought gifts, and purchased Indian clothing, baggy pants, a loose flowing shirt, and vest. When I got on the plane two days later, I noted that all the men wore Western-style suits or jeans and T-shirts. I was the only male on the plane dressed in a traditional Indian outfit. Dan would have appreciated my costume.

About the time I boarded the plane, Dan was loading Sam and Raika on a rental truck. He traveled with them from Jaipur back to Bikaner where we had originally purchased them. When he arrived, there was a welcoming committee. GB and Humper were waiting. Bubbles hadn't sold them yet, thinking it would be best to wait for Dan's return. After some rest and relaxation, and a bill of good health from a veterinarian, the camels were sold to local farmers. Dan and I had previously discussed what to do with the cash from the sale. It was donated to a school that Bubbles was building for desert children.

Sitting on the plane, I thought about the question asked by my traveling companion on the bus, "Does the earth have rights?" I wondered if that included the earth's creatures. Did our camels have their own pages in the book? Would they tell stories of our adventure to their children? I wondered if they would even remember us. I got a partial answer to this last question. Several weeks after the expedition, Dan returned to Bikaner and looked up GB. When he went to the farm where she was living, she immediately went to him and started nuzzling. I like to think that Sam, Raika, and Humper will remember us as well. I know we will remember them.

Epilogue 2

Two years after the India expedition, Dan and I started preparing for our next adventure together. The plan is to explore Mongolia's Gobi Desert on two-humped Bactrian camels.

Appendices

APPENDIX A:

The Fastest Way To Learn a Foreign Language

If you want to be a world-class adventurer, it is a good idea to be able to speak the languages of the countries you travel to. You don't have to be fluent, but knowing 100 to 200 basic words, like *bathroom* or *water*, allows you to communicate. This ability to communicate helped Dan and me to ask directions, make purchases, make friends—and may just have saved our lives in those sticky situations.

As both a high school and university student, I didn't find it difficult to learn a foreign language. I found it impossible. In high school I floundered through French. At university I took a foreign language—only because it was required—and earned the worst grades of my academic career. My experience convinced me that I was a language dunce. That part of my brain was missing. Then I discovered a method used by top language experts. This method appears in more detail in my book, *Memory Smart*. Here's a beginner's introduction to the fastest way to learn a foreign language.

The Say, See, Stick Method for Learning a Foreign Language

The technique I used to memorize Hindi for our trip across India is called the *Say, See, Stick* method. A version of this technique is used by Barry Faber, a man who speaks twenty-five foreign languages including French, Russian, Chinese, Norwegian, Indonesian, Hungarian, Spanish, and Dutch. Using this technique it is possible to learn a hundred or more words in a weekend. Here's how you would use the method to learn the Hindi word for water, pronounced PAN-ee (the actual spelling in Hindi is different because there are different characters in the Hindi alphabet. The spelling you see here is a phonetic spelling; in other words, we are using English letters that approximate what it would sound like in Hindi).

SAY	SEE	STICK
Say PAN-ee out loud several times. Say it slowly and break it down into syllables—PAN-ee. As you say PAN-ee, listen for syllables that sound like English words.	The first syllable of PAN-ee is the English word pan. Visualize a pan. The pan is something that you can see. Close your eyes and imagine a pan.	Now stick the image you have created, the pan, to the meaning of the foreign word. The meaning of PAN-ee is water. Imagine a pan holding water.

Remembering the Word You Just Learned

To retrieve a foreign vocabulary word from your memory, first go to the image that the word represents. If you are looking for the Hindi word for water:

- Imagine water.
- Next, ask, "What image did I stick or associate with the water?" In this case, the image is a pan holding water.
- The image of the pan prompts you to say, PAN-ee, the correct pronunciation for water in Hindi.

Here's the Hindi name for one of the creatures we met on our trip. In Hindi, the word for cobra is pronounced NAG.

SAY	SEE	STICK
Say NAG out loud. Does it sound like an English word you are already familiar with?	NAG sounds like the English word for an old, run-down horse. Imagine a really old horse with a sway back.	Now stick the image you have created, the horse, to the meaning of the Hindi word. The meaning of NAG is cobra. Imagine a cobra riding a nag.

Does This Seem Like a Lot of Work?

If this seems difficult, consider this. Two groups of students were taught a foreign language. One group used the conventional method of learning. Another group used the *Say, See, Stick* method. Conventional techniques improved the students' learning by 24 percent while the *Say, See, Stick* method improved students' learning by 69 percent. You be the judge.

Your Hindi Word List

Now that you understand how *Say, See, Stick* works, here's a list of twelve Hindi words. The first word under the picture is how you pronounce the word in Hindi. The word in bold type indicates the meaning of the Hindi word. The word in italic type is the English sound-a-like. The picture is the memory device that connects the two together.

Give it a try. You may be surprised to find that learning a foreign language is not as difficult as they made it in school.

CHI-ri-yah
Bird carrying *Cheerio*

NAG
Cobra riding a *nag*

bi-STAR
Bed with *big star*

dur-VA-za
Door in a *door vase*

ANKH
Eyes in *anchor*

BARF
Ice *barf*

TANG
Leg sprinkled with *Tang*

MOOH
Cow *mooing* in **mouth**

RAT
Rat out at **night**

cha-VUL
A *shovel* under **rice**

PAN-ee
Water in *pan*

pa-KA-na
Pack on a **toilet**

APPENDIX B:
100 Goals for the Expedition

Years ago I read a story in *Life* magazine that changed my life. The story was about John Goddard, the first explorer to paddle a kayak the full length of the Nile River. It was an awesome adventure in which he was chased by river bandits, escaped from crocodiles, and paddled through flooded tombs. At the end of the story was the part that changed my life. It said that when he was a teen John wrote down 127 goals to complete in his lifetime. Exploring the Nile River was on that list along with landing a plane on an aircraft carrier, publishing an article in *National Geographic,* and climbing Kilimanjaro. In 1995 he had completed 109 of his original goals. Inspired by his example I started my own goal list. One of my goals was to meet John Goddard. When I finally met him, I was even more amazed. I found out that he made a list of new goals every year. These new goals included flying the Goodyear blimp, producing TV documentaries, riding an orca whale, and mushing a dog sled team. When I saw some of the accomplishments on these additional lists I was stunned with how rich a goal-setter's life could be.

Riding camels across India was one of the goals on my list. Knowing the power of goal-setting, I made a separate list of goals to accomplish on this adventure. Here are 100 goals I set for the India expedition. You can find out more about my goal-setting process in the book, *Goal Express! The five secrets of goal-setting success.*

A checkmark indicates completion of that goal.

Things
1. ✓Buy four camels
2. ✓Buy a camel saddle
3. ✓Wear a turban
4. ✓Buy a Lumileds one-watt flashlight
5. Bring home a Tibetan prayer flag
6. Buy a gurka knife
7. Get a Tibetan Thangka scroll painting
8. ✓Have pants and shirt made in India
9. Get a mask in Nepal

Places to visit

10.   ✓Rat temple at Deshnoke (India)
11.   ✓Sariska Tiger Reserve (India)
12.   ✓Jantar Mantar Observatory (India)
13.   ✓Red Fort (India)
14.   Palace of fifty-five windows (Bhaktapur, Nepal)
15.   Keoladeo Ghana National Park and Bird Sanctuary (India)

Experiences

16.   ✓Ride an elephant
17.   ✓Gallop on a camel
18.   ✓Get a camel blessed
19.   ✓Take Ellen (my wife) to a Nepalese restaurant in the States
20.   Watch sunrise over Mt. Everest
21.   Pet a mongoose
22.   ✓Ride a train in India
23.   ✓Ride together with Griffin (my son) on a camel
24.   Ride together with Ellen (my wife) on a camel
25.   ✓Ride camels through Sariska Tiger Reserve
26.   ✓Replace a camel nose peg
27.   ✓Ride a camel under a full moon
28.   ✓Meet an untouchable
29.   ✓Meet a Brahmin
30.   ✓Meet a sadhu holy man
31.   Cross a suspension bridge in Nepal or Tibet
32.   Wade a camel across a stream
33.   Spin a prayer wheel in Tibet
34.   ✓Clicker train a camel
35.   Pull a rickshaw
36.   ✓See a Bollywood movie in India
37.   ✓Read the book *Bandit Queen*
38.   See the movie *Salaam Bombay*
39.   ✓Pay a bribe
40.   Look for the remains of a yeti
41.   ✓Hold a cobra
42.   ✓Eat dal fry

43. Find out if they have a rat patrol in Delhi
44. Take a rowboat out on lake at Keoladeo in early morning
45. ✓Read by the light-in-a-box system we install

Photos

46. Mongoose
47. ✓Indian snake charmer with cobra
48. Dan on a camel with Mt. Everest in the background
49. Tiger
50. Dan next to a Chinese border patrol guard or soldier
51. Yak
52. Jungle Cat
53. Striped Hyena
54. Asian Palm Civet
55. Sloth Bear
56. Golden Jackal
57. Indian Giant Squirrel
58. ✓Hanuman langur
59. ✓Asiatic Elephant
60. Leopard
61. Chital
62. ✓Nilgai
63. Indian Darter
64. Purple Swamp Hen
65. Hoopoe (*Upupa epops*)
66. Golden Tree Snake
67. Russels Viper
68. Ghats and people bathing
69. ✓Spice market
70. Fruit bat
71. Dan on red line on Friendship Bridge (Nepal/Tibet)
72. Flamingo
73. ✓Sambar deer

Things to Learn

74. ✓100 Hindi words

75. Hindi signs for closed, open, men, women
76. ✓Five camel commands in Hindi
77. ✓Snap a bullwhip
78. ✓Circus snap a bullwhip
79. ✓Horizontal snap a bullwhip
80. ✓Overhead snap a bullwhip
81. ✓How to pack a camel
82. ✓How to charm a cobra

Things to do

83. Braid a camel hair bracelet
84. ✓Make a list of 100 goals for the trip
85. Fly a kite from a Himalayan peak
86. ✓Hand out LED lights to journalists
87. ✓Cook a meal over a camel-dung fire
88. ✓Install a solar-powered LED light system in India
89. Install a solar-powered LED light system in Nepal
90. Install a solar-powered LED light system in Tibet
91. ✓Perform the following magic tricks for children in the villages we pass through: rope through neck Skip Wilson style, vanishing and reappearing coins, thumb-tip silk vanish, change one bill into another, three-card monte, card clock, shells and pea game
92. ✓Have a journalist write about our camel trip in an Indian paper
93. Have a journalist write about our camel trip in a Nepalese paper
94. Find a beetle for Dan's collection for the Natural History Museum in London
95. ✓Send pictures and a write up of our adventure to school children in the U.S. during the course of the trip via Internet
96. ✓Make a graphic for the expedition
97. ✓Get a T-shirt with a graphic for the expedition
98. ✓Write a book about the adventure

Personal Traits

99. ✓ Maintain a sense of humor for the duration of the trip by smiling and commenting on the good things that happen
100. Create a target word and visualization to use if I'm feeling frustrated

I had one hundred goals for the Indian adventure. Number sixteen on the list was to ride an elephant. In Jaipur I met Sirkahn and his elephant, Muni. I rode Muni down the city streets and back to Sirkahn's home where he is preparing to remove Muni's saddle.

APPENDIX C:

Breaking a BHAG (Big Huge Awesome Goal) into PGs (Puny Goals)

Starting out on a big huge awesome goal (BHAG) can seem like an overwhelming task. But all BHAGs are made up of puny goals (PGs). If you break a BHAG into PGs it doesn't look so daunting.

Here's what the beginning of the camel adventure, a BHAG, looked like broken down into PGs. The most important step in beginning any goal is to find a PG that you can start working on right away. I began with book research, surfed over to the Internet, then began calculating a budget . . . .

Book research

Internet research

Look for sponsors

Write goals for trip

Find camel seller

Budget

Physical training

Map research

Send letters to sponsors

Immunizations

Camel-riding lessons

Learn how to train camels

Reading basic Hindi
(Translation: Beware of dog)

A musician on the steps of the Amber Fort in Jaipur.

Bibliography

Allerton, Mark. *Hindi in Three Months: Simplified Language Course.* New York: A DK Publishing Book, 1999.

Bergin, Tom. *In the Steps of Burke and Wills.* Australian Broadcasting Commission, 1981.

Bulliet, Richard W. *The Camel and the Wheel.* New York: Columbia University Press, 1990.

Davidson, Robyn. *Desert Places.* Viking, 1996.

Davidson, Robyn. *Tracks.* Vintage, 1995.

Delacy, Richard. *Hindi and Urdu Phrasebook.* Victoria, Australia: Lonely Planet Publications, 1998.

Hardy, Justine. *Scoop Wallah, Life on a Delhi Daily.* London: John Murray, Albemarle ST, 1999.

Kohler-Rollerfson, Llse; Mundy, Paul; and Mathias, Evelyn, editors. *A Field Manual of Camel Diseases: Traditional and Modern Health Care for the Dromedary.* London: ITDG Publishing, 2001.

Kurland, Alexandra. *Clicker Training for Your Horse.* Ringpress Books, 2001.

O'Reilly, James and Habegger, Larry, editors. *Traveler's Tales India: True Stories.* San Francisco Traveler's Tales, 2004.

Pryor, Karen. *Don't Shoot the Dog: The new art of teaching and training.* New York: Bantam Books, 1999.

Sen, Mala. India's *Bandit Queen.* HarperCollins, 2001.

Index

A

B

C

Acknowledgments

First, thanks to Visvajeet "Bubbles" Singh, who went far out of his way to help two adventurers. Gary and Diane Jackson, owners of The Nevada Camel Company, introduced me to camels and allowed me to practice clicker-training skills on four camels: Laverne, Chewie, Milagro, and my nemesis, Saddam. Dr. Dave Irvine-Halliday, head of the *Light Up the World Foundation*, provided the "light-in-a-box" system that we installed at Dwar Mala, India, and information on solar panels and LEDs. Dr. Mehta of the Bikaner Camel Research Station introduced us to buying camels in India. Technical support was provided by Dr. Murray Fowler, retired professor of exotic animal studies at the University of California at Davis. Dr. T.K. Gahlot, at the College of Veterinary and Animal Science in Bikaner, helped us assemble a camel first aid kit. Karen Pryor was kind enough to invite me to my first clicker-training expo where I met Alexandra Kurland who graciously provided us with her clicker-training videos and books. My friend Dr. Peter Ward acted as the expedition's medical liaison and outfitted us with medical supplies. Patti Segraves at Iridium Satellite provided us with an Iridium Satellite phone, our communications link to the world. Joe Martin at Panasonic provided us with a Toughbook Computer for the trip. Christopher Moehrke at Adobe Systems, Inc., donated the software necessary to maintain our web site. Patrick Lavache at Discotechs helped out with our web site and journal maintenance. Dana Hayse coordinated our email and school interest in the expedition. Pelican Boxes gave us cases that kept our delicate equipment intact. Malcolm Vetterlein, at Badbags, donated duffle bags that survived the trip. Ex Officio outfitted us in Buzz Off clothing to ward off mosquitoes. John Schaffer at Real Goods made sure we got the right solar recharging equipment for the field. Mountain Safety Research provided discounts on camping equipment. Financial support for the trip was provided by Tom Cooper, Tom Kelley, Steve Rasmussen, Pamela Rogers, and a donor who wished to remain anonymous. Thanks to the reader families who offered comments on the early drafts of the book: Arima, Bronwer, Dokidis, Fonda, Ganapathy, Grossman, Hopfenberg, Landolifi, Meyers, Novack, Wicks, Zanutta, and Diana Morley who came out of retirement to proof the book. And to my favorite adventurers, Ellen McNeil, my beloved wife and friend, and Griffin Wiltens, the best son a father could have.

About the Author

I live with my wife and son in Redwood City, California. My adventures include being marooned on a deserted island off the coast of Canada, cave diving in the cenotes of Mexico's Yucatan Peninsula in search of ancient human skeletons, kayaking through head hunter territory in Ecuador, summitting Aconcagua in Argentina, tracking big game in Africa, and paragliding off the caldera of an extinct volcano in Mexico. I have written six books, including *Goal Express! The Five Secrets of Goal-Setting Success* and *Memory Smart: Nine Memory Skills Every Grade Schooler Needs*.

During the school year, I work with children in Gifted and Talented Education (GATE) programs in school districts throughout California as well as present workshops for corporate groups such as Google and academic institutions such as Stanford University. For twenty-five years I've spent my summers in the high Sierra mountains directing Deer Crossing Camp, a wilderness summer camp for children that has instruction in everything from white water kayaking to technical rock climbing. Past occupations have included coaching a championship university water polo team, working as head chemist of a Silicon Valley company, writing an award-winning column for the *Bay Area Parent* news magazine, and doing research in marine biology in California, Canada, and Hawaii. One of my favorite quotes is from David Curtis, "We are what we are, and where we are, because we have first imagined it."

To Find Out More

To find out more about corporate and academic programs delivered by Jim Wiltens, as well as other books he has written, go to:

www.jimwiltens.com

Information on Deer Crossing Camp, the summer camp Jim owns and directs, can be found at:

www.deercrossingcamp.com

For additional information on Dan and Jim's trip across India as well as updates on their upcoming adventures together, go to:

www.thecaravanoflight.com